The Morning Star

Vol. 6 ◆ JOURNAL ◆ **No. 4**

© 1996 by MorningStar Publications, Inc. All Rights Reserved.
Editor: Rick Joyner
Contributing Editors: Jack Deere, Francis Frangipane
and Dudley Hall
General Editor: Steve Thompson
Managing Editor: Dianne C. Thomas
Copy Editors: Terri Herrera, Trisha Doran, Dee Davis & Lynn Williams
Production Assistant: Carol Coan, Rainbow Cowan

The Morning Star Journal is published quarterly, 4 issues per year, by *MorningStar Publications, Inc.*, 16000 Lancaster Highway, Charlotte, NC 28277-2061. Fall-1996 issue. Periodicals, Charlotte, NC and additional mailing offices, 10832122-ISSN.

POSTMASTER: Send address corrections to *The Morning Star Journal,* 16000 Lancaster Highway, Charlotte, NC 28277-2061.
Subscription Rates: One year $12.95; Outside U.S. $20.00USD.

MorningStar Publications is a non-profit organization dedicated to the promulgation of important teachings and timely prophetic messages to the church. We also attempt to promote interchange between the different streams, emphases and denominations in the body of Christ.

To receive a subscription to *The Morning Star Journal,* send payment along with your name and address to *MorningStar Publications,* 16000 Lancaster Highway, Charlotte, NC 28277-2061, (704) 542-0278 (1-800-542-0278—Orders Only); fax (704) 542-0280. One year (4 quarterly issues) U.S. $12.95; Outside U.S. $20.00USD. Prices are subject to change without notice.

Reprints. Photocopies of any part of the contents of this publication may be made freely. However, to re-typeset information, permission must be requested in writing from *MorningStar Publications,* 16000 Lancaster Highway, Charlotte, NC 28277-2061.

Kingdom Principles

by T. D. Hall

All Scripture references
NKJV unless otherwise indicated.

When the disciples asked Jesus to teach them to pray, He gave them what we now call "the Lord's prayer." This is the model prayer which is filled with insight, but I want to focus this study on just one phrase in it—"**Thy kingdom come. Thy will be done on earth, as it is in heaven**" (**Matthew 6:10 KJV**). For nearly two thousand years now, the true disciples of Jesus have been praying for His kingdom to come and prevail on the earth just as it does in heaven. It certainly behooves us to understand the emphasis the Lord has given to this one issue.

The Lord Jesus devoted almost His entire ministry to explaining and demonstrating the nature of the kingdom, while saying very little about the church. The Bible actually has much more to say about the kingdom of God than it does the church. Jesus never told us to preach the church, but He told us many times to preach the kingdom of God. This is not to detract from the importance of the church, but there is a difference between the church and the kingdom. Could it be that if we focused as much of our attention upon the kingdom of God as the Lord did that the church might be more likely to become what God has called us to be?

In order to understand the kingdom, we must first recognize that biblically there are only two kingdoms: the kingdom of God and the kingdom of Satan. The Lord gave the better part of His ministry to explaining the dimensions of God's kingdom so that we can abide in it. He also made it clear that if we are not inside the gate, or dimensions of His kingdom, we are outside of His domain. Many have tried to create a third kingdom, their own little kingdoms, where they maintain dominion over their own lives, but we are either submitted to God and His kingdom or the Devil's—there is no "middle kingdom."

The kingdom is not hard to understand, but to do so we need to look at four things: What is the kingdom? Where is the kingdom? When is the kingdom? And how does the kingdom come? If we will answer these questions in order, we will begin to get a clear picture of this most important issue.

What is the kingdom of God? We distinguish an earthly kingdom as the place where the king's will is obeyed. The kingdom of God is simply where the Lord's will is done—as Jesus prayed "Thy kingdom come, Thy will be done." To know what the kingdom of God is, we must know what the Lord's will is. This is the first issue with the kingdom—knowing the Lord's will and doing it.

Where is the kingdom of God? Jesus prayed for the kingdom to come, "On earth as it is in heaven." The kingdom of God is *where* God's will is done. There would be no kingdom if there was no king. A king would not be a real king if his will was not obeyed. This is where there is often a difference between what may qualify as a church, or a congregation of believers, and that which is really a part of the kingdom. There are many churches that may do many wonderful things, but still are not really doing the will of the king. A kingdom has a king who has dominion. Does Jesus really have dominion in our church? Does He really have dominion in our own lives, or is He merely an appendage to our lives that we may occasionally, out of duty, give some attention to? We are only a part of the kingdom of God if God rules in our lives.

Certainly the church is called to be a part of the kingdom of God; she is called to be an instrument of the kingdom. In essence, Jesus said to the church, "When you are under My authority I will give you my authority, and My power to be ambassadors for My kingdom. Use it to extend the limits of My domain so that My will be done on earth just as it is in heaven. You can spread the kingdom of God."

The Lord made an issue of His kingdom coming to earth just as (in like manner) it is established in heaven. Does the Devil have victory over heaven? Of course not! Does the Devil have victory over our lives? If he does, then God is not reigning in our lives like He is in heaven. Does the Devil have victory over our church? Then the Lord is not ruling over our church like He does in heaven. The degree to which the Devil can have his will done in our lives or in our church is the degree to which we are still outside of the domain of the Lord. This leads us to the next question.

When does the kingdom come? That has been the question of the ages. Some people say, "Well, that was back yonder when." Other people say, "It's out yonder someday." It was years before I heard anything except, "In the sweet by and by" or "On Jordan's stormy banks I stand."

But the good news of the kingdom is that you're not standing on any stormy banks of Jordan—you're already there in the promised land! Jesus said that the kingdom was *now*. "Repent! For the kingdom of God is now!" Jesus said. "It's at hand!" When did He say that? That was after God anointed Him to do His ministry. Jesus said that He came to preach the gospel to the poor, to heal the broken-hearted, to set the captive free, to set at liberty those which are bruised, to preach the acceptable year of the Lord. He said, "I've been anointed by the Father to do this! I'm the Messiah, I have come! And the kingdom of God is at hand."

When God starts something, He gets it done. God started out with a man, intending for that man to rule and have dominion on earth. When the Devil tempted man, and man sinned, it didn't stop God. He just said, "We'll cover that sin with the blood. We'll have a Messiah come and He'll do what the first man didn't do." And God sent Jesus. Everything that Adam came and messed up, Jesus came to fix up. And everything that Adam didn't do, Jesus did do. He lived up to every requirement, He passed every test, He overcame the Devil. The Devil had taken over the power and dominion that God had given to Adam—but Jesus came to take it back. Jesus came to destroy the works of the Devil. And that's the reason He said, "The kingdom of heaven is now. I've come to do it." Jesus reclaimed the power and dominion. When He died and rose from the grave, Scripture tells us that He trampled the Devil and the demons under His feet. *All* are submissive to the Lord Jesus Christ. That's good news!

As a believer, you have been given power and authority in Jesus' name to trample down everything the Devil brings up. And you can reign as kings and queens *today* in the name of Jesus—all because Jesus came to take over. That's good news!

Look at Matthew 10:7-8. Jesus said, **"As you go, preach, saying, 'The kingdom of heaven is at hand' "** (NAS). Do you say much about that as you walk through life? We need to tell people that the kingdom of heaven is *now*. The reward of coming to Jesus is that you get in on a kingdom right then. You don't have to wait until you die. That's good news. The eighth verse says, **"Heal the sick, raise the dead, cleanse the lepers, cast out demons; freely you have received, freely give."** That's what the kingdom of God does.

So how does one become a part of the kingdom? Matthew 11:12 says, **"The kingdom of heaven suffers violence, and violent men take it by force"** (NAS). You don't get in on the kingdom of heaven by going to conferences and churches and "amening" the pastor when he preaches. Getting in on the kingdom happens when

you hear something that is available for kingdom people and you say, "I'll take that," and you grab it for yourself. We must have an "I want that" mentality.

When I look at being filled with the Holy Spirit, I must realize that it's not a good *idea*, it's a good *experience*. And I must decide, yes, I want that! When Jesus says that the kingdom of heaven is to have power and authority, I want that! When Jesus says that the kingdom of heaven is having the gifts of the Spirit, I want that! Men and women who aggressively take hold of the realities of the kingdom are the ones who get in on it. I'm talking about men and women who will claim it and say, "The kingdom of heaven is for me because I've been born again." Jesus said if you're born again you can see the kingdom of God.

But where is the kingdom? It's in us. It's in us now. It's the King ruling in your life—NOW. It's His authority in us—NOW. His power in us—NOW. His will being done in us—NOW. The kingdom is in your life because He provided it for you. It's Christ in you, the hope of glory. It's Jesus' life flowing in you. And that's the reason to pray, "Thy kingdom come, Thy will be done. Thy kingdom be done in my life now as it is in heaven, Lord, whatever You have planned in heaven for my life, let it be lived out in my life NOW."

In Matthew 13, Jesus had much to say about the kingdom of heaven and how it works. Here are some things to look for in Scripture as you study the kingdom. First, *the kingdom of heaven is concerned with life.* His kingdom doesn't produce death, it produces life.

The second word to look for is *growth*. When you think about the kingdom there is growth. Another word I want you to look for in Scripture is light or *revelation*. You can't teach the kingdom, nor can you teach people how to get saved. You can *tell* them, but the Holy Spirit of God has to reveal it—the light has to come on. It's the same with any spiritual truth. You're not going to understand the kingdom of heaven until revelation comes. After revelation there comes an action, and after action, there comes a harvest or fruit.

Let's look at the parables in Matthew 13, but let's start backwards at verse 11: **"He answered and said to them, 'Because it has been given to you to know the mysteries of the kingdom of heaven . . .' "** Jesus was sharing these parables so we could understand the mysteries of the kingdom. Let's try to find the main truth of each one of them.

In the parable of the sower, Jesus was teaching *life*—how life in the kingdom happens. He said in verses 3-6,

> **Behold, a sower went out to sow.**
>
> **And as he sowed, some seed fell by the wayside; and the birds came and devoured them.**
>
> **Some fell on stony places, where they did not have much earth; and they immediately sprang up because they had no depth of earth.**
>
> **But when the sun was up they were scorched, and because they had no root they withered away.**

Notice in verse 5 it says **"they sprang up"**—they were planted and they sprang up to life. Verses 8-9 say, **"But others fell on good ground and yielded a crop; some a hundredfold, some sixty, some thirty. He who has ears to hear, let him hear!"**

Jesus explained it when He said,

> **Therefore hear the parable of the sower:**
>
> **When anyone hears the word of the kingdom, and does not understand *it*, then the wicked *one* comes and snatches away what was sown in his heart. This is he who received seed by the wayside.**
>
> **But he who received the seed on stony places, this is he who hears the word and immediately receives it with joy;**
>
> **yet he has no root in himself, but endures only for a while. For when tribulation or persecution arises because of the word, immediately he stumbles.**
>
> **Now he who received seed among the thorns is he who hears the word, and the cares of this world and the deceitfulness of riches choke the word, and he becomes unfruitful.**
>
> **But [*now here is the heart of the parable*] he who received seed on the good ground is he who hears the word and understands it [*and because of that he acts on it and life comes and grows and brings forth fruit*] (Matthew 13:18-23).**

Do you see what Jesus was saying? That's how the kingdom of God works. Hearing, receiving, understanding, acting, fruit.

In chapter 13, verses 24-43, Jesus gave a parable about the tares. If you'll remember, one went out to sow and someone else came and planted some tares in with the wheat. In the first parable, Jesus was talking about the seed being the Word of God sown in the hearts of good soil. That's how people get born in the kingdom of God—when the seed falls in good soil. Now the kingdom of heaven is the soil. And there is power in that soil, but there is power in that seed as well. Did you ever think about how much power and authority there is in the seed? You can lay it down and it will do nothing. But if you get it in the right place it becomes life and becomes a stalk of corn, or cotton, or peanuts. The seed becomes life and grows and produces fruit.

So where is the most power and authority? Is it in the one that plants it or is it in the seed? *The planter is the church, the seed is the word of God, the soil is the kingdom of heaven.* Life and growth are not even dependent on the motivation of how you do it. For instance, I grew up on a farm in south Alabama, and my Dad had a philosophy that you ought to be in the field at daylight. Sometimes my attitude was not too good when I planted seed, but crops would come up anyway.

I remember one time my Dad told me to watch the hopper and keep it from stopping up. But I was more interested in keeping up with the hopper in front of me and I let mine stop up. So I got in there and dug it out and pecks of peanuts came out. Now I knew that if I tried to replant all those peanuts properly I'd get so far behind, I'd never catch up with the hopper running in front of me. So I just covered them up in one big pile. But I had covered up my sins.

A couple of weeks later we were out because Dad liked to go see how the peanuts were coming up. And if they weren't coming up, he'd dig to see what was wrong. I saw him down where I'd messed up and he was digging because there were no peanuts there. Finally he dug till he found a bunch of peanuts all in one wad. I realized that I hadn't planted them with good motives, but the peanuts were growing anyway.

In the same way, we don't have to judge churches by how they do things. One church may not have everything that the church you go to has, but if they get the seed planted in good soil, then kingdom life results. There is power and authority in the soil and in the seed. But when we understand the principles of how it works and we learn to do it right, then we get the right seed, at the right time, at the right place, and we've got a good harvest. The church is in the business of learning how to be part of the kingdom.

In Matthew 13, verses 31-32, we see another parable that Jesus put to them.

The kingdom of heaven is like a mustard seed, which a man took and sowed in his field,

which indeed is the least of all the seeds; but when it is grown it is greater than the herbs and becomes a tree, so that the birds of the air come and nest in its branches.

The kingdom of heaven is growing!

Today the greatest single deterrent to knowledge of Jesus is His familiarity. Because we think we know Him we pass Him by.
Winifred Kirkland

When you see the kingdom of heaven free in your life, then—like a mustard seed—it's going to grow into a big tree. And the failure of a few people griping and fussing about carpet and pianos is not going to change it—the kingdom of God is going to grow. They may try to hinder it, but it's going to grow! No matter how little your seed is, God intends to get the tree out of you. Isn't that encouraging? That's the kingdom of heaven.

Then Jesus gave another parable. He said, "The kingdom of heaven is like leaven. . ."; put a little in and it leavens the whole lump. Now some of you are living in homes where there are no other Christians, but you can leaven the whole lump. You can change your home, you can change the destination of future generations from your family. That's exciting. And it's not because of *your* power, but because you have a seed that's powerful and you have soil that's powerful and you have power and authority given to you by Jesus. You can use the name of Jesus without ever understanding how it works and it's still powerful. If you know the principles of the kingdom you can use them whether you understand them or not. Just say, "Thy kingdom come on earth as it is in heaven," and start joining in with the principles of the kingdom—then you will see life and growth.

Now look at verse 44: **"Again, the kingdom of heaven is like treasure hidden in a field, which a man found and hid: and for joy over it he goes and sells all that he has and buys that field."** Did you ever think about the kingdom of heaven being like a treasure you found? That's what happened to me. *The kingdom is a revelation.* Jesus said, "When he *found* it." When you understand some truth about the kingdom it's going to spur you on to action! What did this man do? He went to cash in all his saving bonds so he could buy it. "He goes and sells all that he has . . ." What he saw motivated him.

The Pearl of Great Price

If you've seen the kingdom, you are motivated to go and give up some things in order to have it. This man found it, went and sold everything he had, and came back to buy it. There are some things worth giving up in order to have the kingdom of heaven.

The next parable is so much like this one (verses 45-46):

> **Again, the kingdom of heaven is like a merchant seeking beautiful pearls,**
> **who, when he had found one pearl of great price, went and sold all that he had and bought it.**

Here is a pearl dealer looking for good pearls. Most of us are like that; we're not here fighting the kingdom of God, we're looking for it. We're looking for the best that God has but we haven't all found it yet. The pearl of great price is the King and His kingdom. Jesus says that when you get a revelation of the kingdom you'll sell your other pearls to get *that* pearl.

We would have revival today if we would get into the pearl trading business—if we could just get a glimpse of what God is doing today. God has promised to do a lot, and He has already started. The Berlin Wall has fallen. Revival is breaking out all over the world. In China there's a great move of God going on. People are being healed and saved and even raised from the dead. The authorities are trying to destroy the church with their rules, but there is power and authority in the kingdom of God that's bigger. And like a mustard seed growing into a big tree, the kingdom of God is growing in China. It's growing in Russia. And even in America, in spite of all the difficulties we have here—the materialism, the attitudes of others, the humanism—the kingdom is still growing. And once you understand the kingdom, the attitudes of others cannot stop you. You'll sell those other pearls to get that pearl of great price. And then you're ready to aggressively take the kingdom of heaven wherever you go.

All of us have pearls that need to be traded. With some of you it's tradition that's a precious pearl to you. But when you get a vision of the kingdom, you realize that you can't have the traditions and the kingdom: you're going to have to trade one or the other. But after a glimpse of the kingdom it won't be hard to know which to trade.

For some of you it's theology. You see something in the Word, but you've always believed something else. But if you want to flow in the kingdom, you'll have to go with the Word—not what you've been told about the Word. For some of you, your pearl will be comfort. You're not comfortable with some new expression. But is the new a part of the kingdom? If it is, trade that old pearl of comfort and security.

For some of you it may be opinions, or it could be possessions. But whatever they are, some of you are going to trade pearls because God is going to show you something better. You're going to trade some pearls to get in on the kingdom. And you're going to be happy about it: you won't be griping.

It bothers me when people give their testimony and tell what they gave up for God. Because you never give up anything that God doesn't repay a hundredfold. You can't out-give God, so if you have a vision of the kingdom, Praise God! He turned the light on and showed you an investment that's worth more than anything else in life. And you will be able to say with confidence, "I gave up this little pearl, but look what He gave me—LOOK WHAT I'VE GOT!"

I am praying that God will turn on the light for all of us so that we will truly see the kingdom. May we all pray together: "Thy kingdom come, Thy will be done, on earth, [in me] as it is in heaven." Amen.

T. D. Hall is currently President of *Emmaus Road Ministry School*, a school offering church leaders and laymen practical training in ministering the works of Jesus. T. D. also serves as Vice President of *Successful Christian Living Ministries* and Director of the *Fellowship of Connected Churches*. He and his wife, Sara, reside in Euless, Texas. They have four children and sixteen grandchildren.

Three from Riches to Rags

BY R. T. KENDALL

All Scripture references KJV unless otherwise indicated.

Throughout human history there has been the repeated phenomenon of someone going "from rags to riches." Less spectacular is that of going "from riches to rags." Moses experienced it when he refused to be known as the son of Pharaoh's daughter, choosing to be mistreated rather than enjoy the "pleasures of sin for a season" (see Hebrews 11:24-25). It was also Joseph's lot, but for a most extraordinary reason.

Joseph was a type of Christ, like many others in the Old Testament. When the Scriptures call one a "type of Christ" it means that their life was a prophetic reflection of the Messiah who was to come, "a shadow of the good things that are coming—not the realities themselves" (Hebrews 10:1 NIV). Many other Old Testament personalities may also be seen as types of Christ. Abel was a type of Christ (see Hebrews 11:4). Isaac, the son of Abraham, was a type of Christ (see Hebrews 11:19). Moses was a type of Christ, as were Joshua, Samuel, David, and the prophets.

The way that Joseph was a type of Christ can be seen in many ways, but at this point we see it particularly in the way he became a victim of his brothers' jealousy and cruelty. It is true that Joseph's brothers' reaction to him was quite natural. You might even say that they couldn't help feeling as they did. But we must nonetheless face the fact that sin was at the bottom of it all. Sin makes all of us want to justify what we do. Sin is inherited from our parents, and the most natural feeling we all have is, "I can't help feeling like I do because I didn't even ask to be in this world." We all have a way of rationalizing sin and trying to explain it away; "I didn't ask to be here. I didn't ask to be a sinner."

This leads us to an apt definition of a Christian: one who takes the responsibility for his own sins and quits blaming his troubles on his parents or upon people or upon society. When that begins to happen and we begin to see that we have got to deal with ourselves, we arc close to becoming a Christian. We must see that we have sinned before God. That is where we must come before we can ever be saved.

The attitude that his brothers had toward Joseph is precisely the way men looked at Jesus. There emerged in the life of Jesus a conspiracy to set him at naught. This happened when Jesus was betrayed by Judas Iscariot. Judas went to the priests of Israel, who took Jesus to Herod, then to Pilate. The whole thing was a conspiracy. Similarly, his brothers saw Joseph coming and said among themselves, **"Let us slay him"** (Genesis 37:20).

But another element in the conspiracy against Joseph was that he was mocked (compare Luke 23:11). When his brothers saw him coming **"they said one to another, Behold, this dreamer cometh"** (Genesis 37:19). Why were they mocking? They were jealous (see Acts 7:9). Even Pontius Pilate knew that the Jews had set Jesus at nought because of jealousy and envy (see Matthew 27:18). They tried to come up with witnesses against Jesus, but they found none.

The next similarity to Christ in the brothers' treatment of Joseph was their cover-up. They said, **"This dreamer cometh. Come now therefore, and let us slay him, and cast him into some pit, and we will say, Some evil beast hath devoured him"** (Genesis 37:19-20). They wanted to cover up what they had decided to do. They would not come to their father and tell the truth. They would say, "Some evil beast hath devoured him."

Once you deliberately bring yourself to commit sin you will need a second sin, a lie, to cover up the first. Sin always leads to lying. This is also what happened in the case of the conspiracy against Jesus. False witnesses were brought in (see Matthew 26:59). They wanted to cover up their own hostility, their jealousy and their motives; so they brought in false witnesses. But you can succeed in a cover-up process only for so long: **"Be sure your sin will find you out"** (Numbers 32:23).

Another sin of Joseph's brothers was their attempt at self justification. The desire to clear ourselves is a fault we all have. They said, **"We shall see what will become of his dreams"** (Genesis 37:20). These brothers regarded their conspiracy to set Joseph at nought as entirely justified. Why? Because Joseph's dreams suggested predestination. If you can abort predestination, you have proved the dream was not really from God. Joseph had obviously believed his dream: "I have dreamed a dream, it will be fulfilled, therefore, you are going to bow down to me." So the brothers wanted to destroy Joseph to show that his dreams were false. This is the way they justified everything that they did. They said, **"We shall see what will become of his dreams."**

And that is the way the Jews looked at Jesus when he was hanging on the cross. They said, **"If thou be the Son of God, come down from the cross"** (Matthew 27:40). They were justifying themselves. They didn't feel guilty about nailing Jesus to the cross. They said, "If Jesus is who he says he is, we don't have anything to worry about: he will just come down from the cross. We will then clap our hands and say 'We're with you, we think you're great; now we believe.' " But when Jesus didn't do that, they were cleared then in their own eyes. This is why men today are so anxious to destroy the Bible; they want to disprove it for the same reasons. "You don't have to worry. There's no need for you to get right with God. The God of the Bible has written a book full of errors so there's no need for you to worry about a heaven or a hell." This is why men love to read an article by a minister who says that the Bible is full of errors.

But there was a similarity in the behavior of the brothers—*respectable neutrality*. Reuben, the eldest brother, heard what the others were planning to do. They were going to kill Joseph and say that some evil beast had devoured him. And Reuben saved Joseph by pulling rank. He was not strong enough physically to stand against the others, so he used his authority as Jacob's firstborn son. Some didn't agree with Christ's death, but they remained "respectably neutral," saying nothing and doing nothing to stop it.

It appears that Reuben had a good motive. He wanted to return Joseph to his father, but all he said was, **"Let us not kill him . . . Shed no blood, but cast him into this pit"** (Genesis 37:21-22). His intention was to go back to the pit later, pull Joseph out, and deliver him to his father. But Reuben did not say what he was going to do. He was ashamed to use his authority to return Joseph then and there. He might have said, "I'm the firstborn. I'm stepping in. You're not going to do that. We're going to return Joseph to our father right now." But he couldn't bring himself to do that. Here was a case of "respectable neutrality." He was convinced that what they were doing was wrong, but he wouldn't come out and stand alone.

Are you like that? In your heart of hearts do you know what is right and what you ought to do? Agrippa said to Paul, **"Almost thou persuadest me to be a Christian"** (Acts 26:28). But the cost was too great for Agrippa to follow Jesus Christ. He was close. Almost there. Reuben didn't agree with what his brothers were going to do, but neither did he have the integrity and courage to deliver Joseph to his father.

Now look at these brothers. They cast Joseph into a pit. Humanly speaking, Joseph could only live a day or two. But that was not

There is today a pale, pathetic, and unflinching interpretation of the blessed gospel, which guarantees salvation as "a financially and socially upgrading experience"; then it finalizes the offer by "a superlative bonus in eternity and comfort world without end." How different was Paul's concept of a disciple of Christ!
— *Leonard Ravenhill*

Obedience which is not voluntary is disobedience.
— *C. H. Spurgeon*

all. These brothers now sat down to eat. How could they do that? They were going to have a meal. They had just left Joseph in a pit without any water. He was going to die in a day or two, and here they were about to eat! I wonder what was in their minds. How could they do it? A hardened conscience lets one do strange things. Now while they were sitting there eating they saw some Ishmaelites coming. Judah, on seeing them, had second thoughts: **"Come, and let us sell him to the Ishmaelites, and let not our hand be upon him; for he is our brother and our flesh"** (Genesis 37:27).

The brothers thought that was a good idea: **"His brethren were content"** (Genesis 37:27). Imagine that! They were actually able to be at peace about selling their brother into slavery! Why? The idea of selling him to the Ishmaelites was mild compared to what they had been prepared to do so that we are told they were *content!* That is an example of the deceitfulness of sin. Do we know what it is to sin so grievously that a lesser sin seems right? That is Satan's deception.

Joseph, who the day before had been in luxury and in security with his coat of many colors, had gone from riches to rags. And that is exactly what happened with Jesus. That is what made Joseph a type of Christ. Joseph went from being wealthy to being emptied, for the ultimate salvation of his brothers—the very ones who persecuted him. Jesus turned his back on the glory of heaven and earth. Though he was God, he thought it not a thing to be grasped, but became man, making himself **"of no reputation"** (Philippians 2:7). **"Foxes have holes, and birds of the air have nests; but the Son of man hath not where to lay his head"** (Luke 9:58). He turned his back on a royal diadem for a crown of thorns. Why did Jesus do that? Why did Jesus go from riches to rags? As Paul put it, **"For ye know the grace of our Lord Jesus Christ, that, though he was rich, yet for your sakes he became poor, that ye through his poverty might be rich"** (II Corinthians 8:9). This Jesus became *nothing*, and it was for us. He died that your conscience and mine could be purged.

So we must not think it strange when we too are called to go through times when we must be emptied, and it seems that all is lost. If we remain faithful to God, it will always work out for our own ultimate exaltation, just as it did for Joseph and Jesus. It will also always work out for the salvation of others.

Minister and author **Dr. R. T. Kendall** was born in Ashland, KY. He graduated from Southern Baptist Theological Seminary in 1972, and The University of Louisville in 1973. Kendall received his doctorate degree in 1977 from Oxford University and became the pastor of Westminster Chapel in London the same year. There he has continued the tradition of challenging the church with a vision that is solidly founded upon an uncommon theological depth and clarity. He has authored 17 books, including the increasingly popular, **"God Meant It For Good"** published by and available through **MorningStar Publications**, and from which this article was excerpted. He and his wife Louise have two children.

As followers of Jesus Christ, our purpose and strength come from our communion with God, not from the Great Commission. God alone is our source, and He must be our focus. Nothing less than full, passionate fellowship with Him will ever empower what we do for Him (see John 15:5).

Something about the occasion of our salvation is important to us. As Christians, we often find special comfort in being able to remember the time and place of our conversion—the specific moment when we passed from death into life. That moment becomes more to us than a tombstone marking our past—it becomes a touchstone, marking the promise of heaven that is yet to come.

So important is the memory of that moment to some that, if for any reason the exact time and date is in question, the "steps" of salvation are repeated. The required words are spoken and the formula is followed again—just to be sure. Sure of what? Sure of heaven. Sure of "being with Jesus someday."

Our Purpose

Victoria Brooks

All Scripture references NAS unless otherwise indicated.

Though the touchstones of our faith are important and used by God in our lives, it seems strange that we look to dates, times, and places to secure a reality that should be living like fire within us. Like a person checking his birth certificate to confirm the beating of his own heart, it's strange that we need to review over and over again our initial steps into the kingdom of God as assurance of our presence there.

Other indicators of life should be evident—something of the very heartbeat of Jesus should echo within us. Something of the inhaling and exhaling of His Spirit with ours should speak to us constantly of our life in Him.

As essential as the moment of our salvation is, the ongoing reality of walking with Jesus should speak to us daily. There is no reason for us to have a greater hope of knowing Christ's presence "someday" in heaven than we do of living in His presence here and now (see Matthew 28:20; John 16:7-15). After all, this is where we met Him. Earth is where He first made Himself real to us. It is here that He told us He would never leave us nor forsake us (see Hebrews 13:5 KJV). Surely it is here, as well as in heaven, that He intends for us to know the reality of His presence.

I grew up reading fairy tales. When I was quite young I was given several large, beautifully illustrated volumes of tales from Russia, China, England, Scandinavia and India. I spent hours with these books piled high around me, reading and re-reading stories of great adventure and romance. Though exciting and varied in plot, the endings were always the same. Somebody good always got the girl and they rode off into the mist, never to be seen again. The story ended and they disappeared. All I knew was that they lived happily ever after.

It is tempting to live this way with Christ. It is tempting, at the point of our salvation, to ride off into an emotional mist and disappear. All is well with us. We have found Jesus and have secured eternal life. We're "safe" and headed for heaven, so what more is there?

In the interim, we're not entirely sure what is expected of us. We know that the Bible speaks of spiritual priesthood, but we don't know what that means in relation to us. We know that we have been called to "abide in Christ," but we're not sure how that's done.

In many ways these things seem mysterious and out of reach. We long for a living intimacy with God and deeply desire a sense of His presence, but are baffled by the resistance we face as we try to find it. How can we approach Him with any confidence of securing the fellowship He offers? We've tried, but with little sense of genuine contact.

Most of us want a deeper interaction with God; we truly desire a more vital, spontaneous exchange of hearts, but have grown accustomed to silence instead. Our prayer times are lonely, our "quiet times" too quiet, and our Bible study, just that—study.

Though we know we will live in God's presence in heaven, we don't know how to live in His presence here on earth. Though convinced that we will sustain great intimacy with Him throughout eternity, we don't know how to attain such closeness here and now.

So, we wait it out. We fix our hope on the next life and expect that a magical, effortless intimacy with God will develop the moment we leave this world behind. Emotionally, we withdraw from the daily demands of relating to Jesus Christ and turn our attention instead to the demands of human need. We do this not because it is our first and truest calling, but because the needs are obvious, tangible and urgent. We can do something in response. We turn our heart toward relationships in which the interactions are "real" and forthcoming, and the results are quantifiable.

The only problem with this approach is that it does not satisfy the deepest desire of God's heart. It does not secure His full pleasure, because it does not account for the full mandate that is on our lives. We were created for fellowship and ministry to God (see Isaiah 56:6-7), not just to the world around us.

Because this is true—because we were brought into being to respond to His heart—God does not allow us to stay safely nestled in a pocket of earthly productivity untouched by intimacy with Him. He pursues us.

My husband and I know a pastor in Illinois who has a large, thriving church. Every week over 2,500 people attend the worship services. He leads a staff of ten associate pastors, presides over care groups, counseling services, and a Christian grade school. His pastorate is clearly marked with the traditional signs of accomplishment and success. There is, however, a deeper, more important ministry that undergirds the obvious, "successful" ministry that most people see.

Ever since he was a child growing up on a farm in central Illinois, this man wanted to be in the ministry—to serve God by serving people. So real was his dream that, as a teenager driving the family tractor, he spent hours preaching to the open fields.

Finally, after completing his education, he and a friend began a small, fledgling congregation. As co-pastor of this new little church, his dream began to take shape. Soon larger and larger crowds were gathering each Sunday morning. The fulfillment of his lifelong ambition seemed on the verge of realization, when suddenly everything came to a crashing halt.

We have been given authority to touch the heart of God.

Through a series of circumstances, God asked this man to give up his pastorate. During times of prayer, he clearly heard the Lord ask him to relinquish all of his work. The exact words God spoke to his heart were, "Would you be willing for Me to put to death your ministry?"

Days and nights of agonized struggle followed. "Lord!" he cried incredulously, "All I've ever wanted to do is be a minister to your people. Everything I've trained for is just beginning to happen. People are getting saved, the church is thriving, I'm preaching well, and hurting people are being helped. I'm doing all this for You! How can You want me to step down now?"

As unbelievable as it seemed, the crushing conviction of God's will grew inside of him until he faced the inevitable question: "Is it the ministry that I love or is it God that I love?"

The two had seemed inseparable. To love God had always meant to serve people. It had always been a foregone conclusion that one begat the other. Now, everything was a tangle of mixed motives and fading dreams. Like an unbroken colt, his heart bucked and reared as it realized the size and weight of the load it was being asked to bear. Heaviness and grief settled on him. All of the fondly held promises for his future were being recalled.

God was demanding the life of this man's Isaac and, like Abraham before him, he responded with an act of worship. He relinquished his pastorate.

"Lord," he said, "I don't understand this; I don't know why You're requiring it of me, but I love You more than I love my ministry, so here it is. I give it back to you. If all I am ever allowed to do in Your kingdom is worship You, it will be enough. If no one ever hears me preach but You, it will be enough. My ministry to You is more important than my ministry to people."

That day, a true "minister of the gospel" was born—someone who ministers to God first and to people second. A year later, God restored this man to the pastorate and now he can look back over twenty-five years of God's continual provision and blessing.

With or without the blessings, however, this man knows he has been marked for life. He will never again be just a successful pastor; he will always be a full-fledged minister. Any weekday morning, before facing the needs of his people, he can be found on his knees in the church prayer room ministering to the heart of his God.

It is true that the task of working to meet human need has been given to the church. The Scriptures are quite clear that we have been commissioned to touch the wounds of the world around us, but that is not all we have been empowered to do. We have been given authority to touch the heart of God. By virtue of our love for God we have been called to stand before Him as those who minister directly to Him (see II Chronicles 29:11).

This is the same authority King David exercised as he ministered to God in the tabernacle. Though not a Levite and, therefore, not a priest, David pursued the presence of God with such tenacity that he was welcomed by God as a friend. For David, ministering to God was not a ritualistic, religious duty; it was an all-consuming way of life.

Long before he played his harp to soothe King Saul, David used it to minister to God in worship. Long before he was allowed to minister to His people as their king, David ministered to God as a hunted exile. Through countless psalms, David the shepherd sang of his Shepherd (see Psalm 23), and David the warrior-king sang of his own invincible Warrior-King (see Psalms 18; 62:1).

We get a clear understanding from Scripture that David's foremost passion was toward the God that he loved and served (see Psalms 25:15; 63:11). Sheep or no sheep, kingdom or no kingdom, David's heart was ever fixed upon his God. Though he was not a priest, by virtue of his worshiping heart David carried a priestly mandate and eventually led all of Israel in ministry to God (see II Samuel 6). So real was his example of active, passionate pursuit of God, that he is known simply by that title; David, **"a man after His [God's] own heart"** (I Samuel 13:14).

Ministering to God was not just David's purpose in life; it was also his protection. By staying close to God in worship, David remained safe from the fear of man (see Psalm 27:1-3). By ministering to God, he became acquainted with God's ways and loyal to His purposes.

This we see evidenced in his battle with Goliath. While fear of man paralyzed the whole of Israel's army, fear of the living God energized David and propelled him to victory in one of the most remarkable battles the world has ever seen (see I Samuel 17:20-51).

King Saul, by contrast, is not presented in Scripture as someone who ministered to God. Instead, he is portrayed as a man so preoccupied with himself that he stayed safely clear of any extravagant, personal interaction with God. His own inadequacy, not God's sufficiency, became the primary focus of his attention.

Though anointed with the Holy Spirit, favored by God with kingship, and entrusted with the welfare of Israel, Saul's anxious, vain heart finally folded in on itself, and he became a tormented, demonized man. Insecure, self-absorbed and afraid, Saul eventually succumbed to the will of the people he ruled instead of to the God that he served (see I Samuel 13:8-14).

By the end of his reign he had no ministerial role in Israel—not to his people, not to his God. In fact, by the end, Saul knew God in only remote, second-hand ways, and it wasn't enough to save his kingdom or his life.

From the lives of these two kings we can draw this conclusion: Regardless of how well-positioned or equipped someone may be to minister to mankind, if they wish to do so in the name of God, they must first know the heart of God. And, if they are to truly know the heart of God, they must put their ministry to Him before all other things.

This is true for every believer, not just for the kings of ancient Israel. All Christians are, by definition, ministers to God first—then to mankind. The Scriptures tell us that the first and greatest commandment is to **"love the LORD your God with all your heart, and with all your mind, and with all your** strength" **(Mark 12:30)**. The second is to **"love your neighbor as yourself" (Mark 12:31)**.

Our ministry to God is eternal in nature and requires the ongoing gift of our heart for the sole purpose of His pleasure. Our ministry to mankind, though important in its own right, must always be the result of our communion with God, never the other way around.

Any work that we do among men, women, and children here on earth must emerge directly from our intimacy with God. Nothing less can sustain it (see John 15:4-7). Any comfort we give, any help we offer, must always be colored by our contact with God's heart. Everything we do to fulfill the second commandment must always pass through the filter of the first.

It follows, then, that though we may find it more convenient to skip the demands of a current, daily interaction with God, He does not. While our own expectations of intimacy may be allowed to slumber until "someday," His never will. His intentions toward us remain compellingly present-tense.

God's heart is not passive as He calls forth His priesthood—those who minister to Him. The fire of His own expectation is not tempered by the passage of time, for He knows there is no reason to wait. All has been accomplished. Everything that is necessary was acquired for us at Calvary. The price was paid, access to His presence was purchased (see Hebrews 10:15-22), and the door stands open for His priesthood to enter.

So it is that God insists on something unique, current and personal from each of us. He requires that who we are interacts with Who He is. He asks for something from us that we can't hang a date on and tuck away in our spiritual hope chest. He wants more than a moment in time when we agreed to His conditions, shook hands, and promised to meet again in heaven.

If it is, therefore, our intention to fill heaven with endless concerts of praise, we start here on earth. If it is we who desire to share the dwelling place of the Most High God, we begin now! If eternity is ours, so is the present!

Now is the time to approach God with courage; now is the time to enter His nearness —here, in this life, without waiting for death to "free" us. For if Jesus is our Savior and Lord, then we have already died with Him and are already free. We are, in fact, by God's own proclamation, **"a royal priesthood, a holy nation" (I Peter 2:9)**, equipped and set apart for Him alone. We minister to the heart of God here and now, not just in the age to come!

Vicki Brooks lives in Cedar Rapids, Iowa, with her husband, Dr. Michael Brooks, and their three sons, Nathan, Jordan and Zion. They attend River of Live Ministries and carry in their hearts a passion for the building up of the body of Christ and the priestly role of each believer as expressed in ministry to God. This article was excerpted from her recently-released book, "Ministering to God: The Reach of the Heart," published by Arrow Publications.

Words of Wisdom from
Dr. Martin Luther King, Jr.

➤ Science investigates; religion interprets. Science gives man knowledge which is power; religion gives man wisdom which is control. Science deals mainly with facts; religion deals mainly with values. The two are not rivals. They are complementary. Science keeps religion from sinking into the valley of crippling irrationalism and paralyzing obscurantism. Religion prevents science from falling into the marsh of obsolete materialism and moral nihilism.

➤ So I say to you, seek God and discover Him and make Him a power in your life. Without Him all of our efforts turn to ashes and our sunrises into darkest nights. Without Him, life is a meaningless drama with the decisive scenes missing. But with Him we are able to rise from the fatigue of despair to the buoyancy of hope. With him we are able to rise from the midnight of desperation to the daybreak of joy. St. Augustine was right—we were made for God and we will be restless until we find rest in Him.

➤ A religion true to its nature must also be concerned about man's social conditions. Religion deals with both earth and heaven, both time and eternity. Religion operates not only on the vertical plane, but also on the horizontal. It seeks not only to integrate men with God, but to integrate men with men and each man with himself. This means, at bottom, that the Christian gospel is a two-way road. On the one hand, it seeks to change the souls of men and thereby unite them with God. On the other hand, it seeks to change the environmental conditions of men so that the soul will have a chance after it is changed. Any religion that professes to be concerned with the souls of men but is not concerned with the slums that damn them, the economic conditions that strangle them, and the social conditions that cripple them, is a dry-as-dust religion. Such a religion is the kind the Marxists like to see—an opiate of the people.

➤ True peace is not merely the absence of tension, it is the presence of justice.

➤ Ultimately you can't reach good ends through evil means, because the means represent the seed and the end represents the tree.

Desperate Dependence

by Bob Sorge

All Scripture references NKJV unless otherwise indicated.

God often takes His servants through the personal distress referred to in Scripture as "the wilderness." God has a clear purpose in mind for this experience. When the wilderness has completed its work in us, we will be broken, humble, and soft with a new fire kindled in our eyes! It will be a fiery love for the One who led us through the wilderness, our beloved Lord and Bridegroom, Jesus Christ.

"Who is this coming up from the wilderness, *leaning* upon her beloved?" (Song of Solomon 8:5). It is the believer who has allowed the wilderness to produce within her an abandoned obedience, a matured love, and a selfless servanthood. The wilderness represents the difficulties of this present world—our struggles with the flesh and temptation; affliction and tribulation; dry seasons in God. "Coming up from the wilderness," she is on the other side of the desert, and her most striking characteristic is this: she is "leaning on her beloved."

The bride in the Song of Solomon represents the pathway of all fervent believers as God brings us into fruitful maturity. By the time she gets to chapter eight, she represents the believer whose love is fully matured. We would expect her to be a spiritual giant, a veritable pillar, standing head and shoulders above others. But no, she can hardly stand up. She has been so broken of her independence by the wilderness experience that she depends upon her Beloved for every step. This is one scriptural depiction of spiritual maturity.

Maturity in Christ is measured by how much we've come to depend on Him. The greater the dependence, the greater the maturity. God is looking for brokenness, helplessness, weakness and dependence upon Him.

Four Kinds of Dependence

We all start out at "total independence." This is the natural state of every unbeliever. Those outside Christ rely exclusively upon their own resources to survive.

Second, there is "claimed dependence." When we first come to Christ we eagerly say, "Lord, I depend completely upon You!" But we're oblivious to the fact that we don't know the first thing yet about dependence. We continue to rely upon the personal support systems we built before we came to Christ.

Then there's "realized dependence." This is what happens when the Lord shows us how utterly dependent we are upon Him, and we embrace the truth that we can do nothing apart from Him (see John 15:5). At this level the believer sincerely cries out to God for help in every area of life.

Finally, there is what I call "desperate dependence." This level of dependence, illustrated in Song of Solomon 8:5, is achieved only through the purposeful formation of the Holy Spirit. He leads us into a wilderness experience that He creates specifically and personally just for us. By the time He's finished with us, we will have learned this ultimate expression of dependence. One indicator that you've come to the place of desperate dependence is this: time spent with Jesus in prayer is no longer a discipline, nor is it merely a delight; prayer (relationship with God) has become for you a matter of sheer survival.

How Jesus Cultivated Dependence

God has a proven method for reducing our self-reliance—He chops us off at the knees. One of the best illustrations for this is Jesus' relationship with His disciples. Look at how He talked to them at times. "You don't know what spirit you are of." "How long will I put up with you?" "Do you still not understand?"

"Oh you of little faith!" Being a disciple of Jesus was real tough on the ego. Many times I've wondered why Jesus was so hard and abrupt with His disciples. I used to think it was because He got upset with them. But then I realized He expected next to nothing of them, so it wasn't a matter of them falling short of His expectations.

So why was the Lord so tough on His disciples? Because they were so full of themselves. They thought they were ready to drink His cup and be baptized with His baptism; they were ready to follow Him to the death; they were ready to sit on His right and left hand in the kingdom of God. They were watching people get healed and delivered under their ministry. They could be so pleased with themselves that it took three years of Jesus' rebukes to cut them down to size. Jesus wanted them to realize their complete bankruptcy apart from Him, so they could be more fruitful.

Peter was probably the toughest nut of the Twelve to crack. To the very end he maintained his self-confidence. When the final test came, Jesus announced to them, "You're all going to flunk tonight." Peter insisted, "Not me, Lord. Maybe the rest of these losers will flunk, but I'll never fail you, Lord." To that Jesus responded, "Simon, you're going to flunk three times tonight!"

I'd always wondered, "Lord, why were you so hard on Peter?" And then I saw it. Unless Peter had been emptied of dependence on himself, he could have never been used on the Day of Pentecost as he was and survived it. If he hadn't been broken, the Day of Pentecost would have turned Peter into a monster. He would have assumed that the harvest of that day had some kind of connection to his powerful preaching. Just imagine how the logo on his business cards might have read: "Three thousand converted at first sermon!" However, God was able to use him at Pentecost and beyond in such a powerful way because he had come to the end of himself, and realized the emptiness of his own resources.

King Hezekiah

One of the most colorful Bible illustrations of this truth is in the story of Hezekiah, king of Judah. Hezekiah was a powerful, godly king (he was discipled by the mighty prophet Isaiah). He purged the land of idolatry, repaired the Temple, and restored proper Temple worship. Then he observed the Passover—nothing like it had happened since the days of Solomon. The priests were once again supported by tithes. Because of his devotion to the Lord, Hezekiah saw one of the greatest deliverances of the entire Bible—185,000 Assyrian enemies were killed overnight by a destroying angel. Hezekiah stands out as one of the most godly kings the nation of Judah had.

Hezekiah illustrates for us the processes God uses to bring His servants into greater dependence. I wish I could say that in Hezekiah's case it worked, but it didn't. Hezekiah is an example of a man who was unwilling to embrace the "desperate dependence" God tried to produce in his heart. As we review Hezekiah's story, we see it is possible to remain loyal in our love for the Lord, but still miss His highest purposes for our life.

During Hezekiah's reign Assyria was the foremost world power. Assyria had captured Samaria, and exiled the Israelites in the northern kingdom back to Nineveh. And now Assyria was knocking on the door of the southern kingdom, the nation of Judah, where Hezekiah was king.

Isaiah 36 and 37 record the Assyrian offensive against Judah. In the crisis of the Assyrian siege, Hezekiah came to a place of "realized dependence." He was fully convinced that God was his only hope, and he cried out to God in desperation for His intervention. Isaiah 37:36 tells how 185,000 dead Assyrians were discovered the next

morning, and the remainder of the enemy's army had returned for Nineveh. It was a glorious deliverance!

But as we come to the next chapter of Isaiah, I can hear God saying, "Okay, Hezekiah, you've done well. You've realized your absolute dependence upon me. You've stayed true to Me in your heart, and you really love Me. Now I'm going to bring you to the greatest test of all. I'm going to see if you're willing to embrace the ultimate level of dependence—desperate dependence." In Isaiah 38:1-5 this ultimate test is introduced:

In those days Hezekiah was sick and near death. And Isaiah the prophet, the son of Amoz, went to him and said to him, "Thus says the LORD: 'Set your house in order, for you shall die and not live.' "

Then Hezekiah turned his face toward the wall, and prayed to the LORD,

and said, "Remember now, O LORD, I pray, how I have walked before You in truth and with a loyal heart, and have done what is good in Your sight." And Hezekiah wept bitterly.

And the word of the LORD came to Isaiah, saying,

"Go and tell Hezekiah, 'Thus says the LORD, the God of David your father: "I have heard your prayer, I have seen your tears; surely I will add to your days fifteen years." ' "

The Furnace of Affliction

Physical affliction is intensely stressful. The crisis that affliction precipitates provides a context where God can reveal the depths of our hearts, and produce a desperation within us that can cause us to seek God with greater fervency. Hezekiah was no exception. The intensity of his trial produced great anxiety of heart and mind, and Isaiah 38:3 says he "wept bitterly." He mourned the loss of the best years of his life (see verse 10). He was about to die in his prime, and so he cried out to God with all his heart.

The Lord heard his prayer, and added fifteen years to his life (see verse 5). After his recovery, he realized that his "great bitterness" was intended by God for his own benefit (see Isaiah 38:17). Hezekiah recognized that God wanted to work something within him through the affliction, but as we'll see, the attempt was unsuccessful.

HERE COMES THE TEST

After Hezekiah's recovery it's as though God says, "All right, Hezekiah, you've come through this fiery trial, and now let's see if it's produced in you the desperate dependence I'm looking for." (After removing the fire from your life, God always tests the gold.) This test comes in the form of envoys from Babylon (see Isaiah 39). The previous test came in the form of an invading Assyrian army, and Hezekiah passed that test. But now this second test comes in the form of smiling ambassadors, and Hezekiah isn't ready for the test to come in such a friendly fashion:

At that time Merodach-Baladan the son of Baladan, king of Babylon, sent letters and a present to Hezekiah, for he heard that he had been sick and had recovered.

And Hezekiah was pleased with them, and showed them the house of his treasures—the silver and gold, the spices and precious ointment, and all his armory—all that was found among his treasures. There was nothing in his house or in all his dominion that Hezekiah did not show them (Isaiah 39:1-2).

Babylon was a pretty powerful nation, and it was quite an honor for such a mighty nation to give Hezekiah this kind of attention. The fact is, Babylon was trying to pull together a political alliance in order to throw off the Assyrian yoke. When Babylon had heard that 185,000 Assyrians had been killed, and that now Hezekiah had recovered from his sickness and was going to be continuing at the helm of the nation of Judah, they sent some ambassadors to strengthen their political ties.

Hezekiah was unable to handle the acclaim that came to him upon his restoration. I can just imagine God's frustration at this moment. It's as though God were thinking, "I really do want to bless you. I want to answer your prayers. I want to heal you. But then when I do, you get proud. It goes to your head, and you start to act as though you deserved it or something." God wants us to get to the place where our souls will be able to steward the attention that His blessing precipitates.

The ambassadors' fawning attention went to Hezekiah's head. He thought to himself, "I

> You have not a continuing city here, and wherever you are, you are a foreigner and pilgrim. Neither shall you ever have rest unless you be most inwardly united unto Christ. Why do you here look about, since this is not the place of your rest? Heaven ought to be your dwell place.
>
> *Thomas á Kempis*

can't believe it, the king of Babylon thinks I'm a force to be reckoned with. He sees me as a world power. I am being courted by the real movers and shakers. I'm really starting to play with the big boys."

God was looking for desperate dependence, but instead, pride began to manifest in Hezekiah's heart. He lost perspective on how the victory over Assyria was an act of God from beginning to end, and how his recovery of health was only God's merciful kindness toward him. Hezekiah may have thought he had mastered this area of dependence upon God, but the right circumstances were used of God to surface the pride of his heart. God knew Hezekiah's heart better than Hezekiah did.

Knowing the Heart

Second Chronicles 32:31 provides a fascinating commentary on this story: **"However, regarding the ambassadors of the princes of Babylon, whom they sent to him to inquire about the wonder that was done in the land, God withdrew from him, in order to test him, that He might know all that was in his heart."**

The translators of the New King James Version capitalize the word "He" in the above phrase, **"that *He* might know all that was in his heart."** But it could just as easily be translated "he," meaning that Hezekiah might know all that was in his heart. God knew what was in Hezekiah's heart all along, but the test came in order that Hezekiah might be able to see it as well.

If he had learned desperate dependence, Hezekiah would not have been seduced by the smiling ambassadors. However, Hezekiah was still impressed with his natural resources—the arm of flesh. Hezekiah had failed the test, indicating that the fiery furnace of affliction did not complete the intended work in Hezekiah's heart. He had not gained the ultimate level of dependence.

The smiling ambassadors got him. When he was under siege by a vast army, it was easy to be dependent upon God. But when his high-powered friends began to fuss over him, the true state of his heart was revealed. The greatest tests of our hearts often come to us not in the face of our enemies, but in the presence of our friends.

A Second Dynamic: An Enlarged Heart

There was a second dynamic in this situation that God was trying to accomplish in Hezekiah: In addition to producing a desperate dependence, God also wanted to enlarge Hezekiah's heart. This is God's design for our lives as well.

An enlarged heart is a heart that has been expanded by God to carry the concerns of others. It has a passion for reaching beyond the concerns and issues that affect our own personal life to embrace the needs of others.

We can see Paul's enlarged heart in his statement of II Corinthians 7:3, **"you are in our hearts, to die together and to live together."** The church at Corinth was only one of many churches Paul had planted, but he related to them in this passage as though they were the most important church in the whole world. Those believers were so much a part of his heart that he felt like his living or dying was inextricably connected to their living or dying.

An enlarged heart is a heart for the world. It is a heart that beats with the passions and concerns of God Himself. What's amazing in Paul's case was his passion, not only for the churches he had planted, but also for his nation, Israel. In Romans 9:1-3, he made the sincere claim that he could wish himself cut off from Christ if it would mean the salvation of his fellow countrymen. Paul carried a passion for both the Gentiles and the Jews.

An enlarged heart is also one that has been given a greater capacity to channel God's love to others. When Paul said to the Philippians, **"For God is my witness, how greatly I long for you all with the affection of Jesus Christ" (Philippians 1:8),** he was basically saying, "The love Jesus has for you fills my heart and flows through me toward you."

God wants to expand our hearts beyond the limited interests of our own sphere of influence. Is my heart heavy when a nearby gospel-preaching church is suffering a loss of members, even when part of me wants to rejoice that those members are now coming to my local church? An enlarged heart finds its interests much broader than the confines of its own ministry involvements. It is free of all jealousy, competition, and comparison.

How God Enlarges Our Hearts

God often uses personal crises to enlarge our hearts. Our hearts often resist God's stretching processes, and usually it takes something very traumatic to work a permanent enlargement of our heart. David cried out, **"The troubles of my heart have enlarged; Bring me out of my distresses!" (Psalm 25:17).** David was learning that God enlarges the troubles of our heart—to enlarge our heart. Although David may have felt ready to lead the nation after killing Goliath, God knew that he needed several years in "the wilderness" to enlarge his heart for the great dynasty He had in store for him.

I am not suggesting that troubles are the only device God uses to enlarge our hearts. Psalm 119:32 makes it clear that radical obedience also contributes to heart enlargement. It is also possible to have our hearts enlarged by receiving a deepening revelation of the love of God. Paul spoke of being constrained to serve others by the love of Christ. But crisis is particularly useful in God's hands for stretching us out of our comfort zones. It's no small thing to take a constricted, self-centered, self-absorbed

Christian and turn him into a world-class Christian. At this point some readers are probably thinking, "So that's why God's been stretching me lately!"

Some Principles Regarding Heart Enlargement

1. *We are incapable of enlarging our own heart.*

   It must be done by the heavenly Surgeon. First Kings 4:29 says that **"God gave Solomon wisdom and . . . largeness of heart."** God does this to leaders because leaders need it. The needs within God's flock are so diverse that His leaders need this enlarging work done in their hearts.

2. *One characteristic of an enlarged heart is deep compassion borne of brokenness.*

   In some this is characterized through weeping and tears. Now, I know some people that are naturally "weepy" because of their personality. But that is not what I'm talking about. I'm talking about a brokenness that is not native to your personality.

   A great example of this is the prophet Jeremiah. The Spirit had warned the people through Jeremiah that their sin would bring God's judgment. But the people of Israel said his words weren't from God. They struck him; they imprisoned him; they put him in a muddy pit where he almost died; and then they abducted him against his will to Egypt. But when the city of Jerusalem finally fell according to Jeremiah's words, did he say, "I told you so"? No. He said, **"My eyes overflow with rivers of water for the destruction of . . . my people" (Lamentations 3:48).** Even after his prophecies of destruction were fulfilled, his enlarged heart won out. Instead of pointing the finger, all he could do was weep.

Paul's enlarged heart was also manifest by the tears that flowed as he cared for the flock. **"Therefore watch, and remember that for three years I did not cease to warn everyone night and day with tears"** (Acts 20:31). An enlarged heart will contain a deep compassion.

We see the largeness of Jesus' heart as He wept over Jerusalem. His words over that great city were, in essence, as follows: "My heart is large enough to gather all of you under My wing, but you would not." In His crucifixion, Jesus demonstrated that the enlarged heart does not just love those who receive it, but it pours out its life for those killing it.

3. *An enlarged heart tastes of divine pleasures.*

Yes, the enlarging of our hearts is a painful process, but in the end it brings a harvest of great glory. An enlarged heart is expanded in its ability to embrace the height and width and length and breadth of Christ's love. And there is nothing like receiving a revelation of Christ's love for you! The enlarged heart shares in the delight of the Master as hundredfold fruitfulness springs forth from our life. In a sublime sense, the enlarged heart also has more fun.

Back to Hezekiah

As a reminder, Isaiah chapters 36 and 37 chronicle the story of the Assyrian invasion of Judah, and how God brought Hezekiah to a place of real dependence on Him. Because Hezekiah relied upon God alone, He brought a tremendous victory over the Assyrians. In the next chapter (Isaiah 38), it's as though God were saying, "Okay, Hezekiah, when your own skin was on the line, you really cried out to Me and saw Me as your only source of help. I'm glad that you seek My face when your life is in the balance. But how about when the lives of others are in the balance? Will you cry out to Me with the same passionate concern for others when their lives are on the line, but yours isn't?"

The nature of Hezekiah's next test is given for us in Isaiah 39:1-8:

At that time Merodach-Baladan the son of Baladan, king of Babylon, sent letters and a present to Hezekiah, for he heard that he had been sick and had recovered.

And Hezekiah was pleased with them, and showed them the house of his treasures—the silver and gold, the spices and precious ointment, and all his armory—all that was found among his treasures. There was nothing in his house or in all his dominion that Hezekiah did not show them.

Then Isaiah the prophet went to King Hezekiah, and said to him, "What did these men say, and from where did they come to you?" So Hezekiah said, "They came to me from a far country, from Babylon."

And he said, "What have they seen in your house?" So Hezekiah answered, "They have seen all that is in my house; there is nothing among my treasures that I have not shown them."

Then Isaiah said to Hezekiah, "Hear the word of the LORD of hosts:

'Behold, the days are coming when all that is in your house, and what your fathers have accumulated until this day, shall be carried to Babylon; nothing shall be left,' says the LORD.

'And they shall take away some of your sons who will descend from you, whom you will beget; and they shall be eunuchs in the palace of the king of Babylon.' "

> So Hezekiah said to Isaiah, "The word of the LORD which you have spoken is good!" For he said, "At least there will be peace and truth in my days."

Hezekiah was a righteous king. He rooted out idolatry; he re-established Temple worship according to Moses' pattern; through his submission he saw 185,000 Assyrians killed in one night! He did a lot for his generation! However, upon examining verses 7-8 above, we see that Hezekiah didn't have a heart for the generations that would follow. When it involved the interests of his own generation, and when it involved his status before his peers, Hezekiah's heart was huge. He cared deeply and dearly for those of his generation. But he lacked a heart for the next generation. His heart was still small for those beyond his field of vision.

A Heart for the Next Generation

Earlier on, God had spoken a most forceful word to Hezekiah through the prophet Isaiah:

> In those days Hezekiah was sick and near death. And Isaiah the prophet, the son of Amoz, went to him and said to him, "Thus says the LORD: Set your house in order, for you shall die and not live' " (Isaiah 38:1).

What was Hezekiah's response to that powerful word of judgment from God? He cried out to God for mercy! God responded to his desperate cry, healed him, and gave him fifteen more years to live.

Now, God comes to Hezekiah a second time with a forceful word of judgment through the prophet Isaiah: "And they shall take away some of your sons who will descend from you, whom you will beget; and they shall be eunuchs in the palace of the king of Babylon" (Isaiah 39:7). What does Hezekiah do in response to this word? Does he cry out for mercy, like he did when it involved his own life? Verse 8 reads: "So Hezekiah said to Isaiah, 'The word of the LORD which you have spoken is good!' For he said, 'At least there will be peace and truth in my days.' "

He doesn't cry out at all. There's no intercession. There are no tears from Hezekiah. God's judgment involved the generations to come, so Hezekiah takes on a passive stance. He basically says, "Well, that's the judgment of God, and who can change God's mind? Since that's what He's spoken, that's what's going to happen. God's going to do what God's going to do."

I can imagine God's disappointment being expressed in thoughts something like these: "Oh, Hezekiah, you missed it! Your life was so insulated that you couldn't really empathize with the hurts of others. After trouble and pain came into your life, to sensitize your heart to the pain of others, you still did not change. I wanted you to embrace a compassion for the heartache of others. But now, when you have the opportunity to be broken over the distress of future generations, you are smug and self-content. You have failed the test, Hezekiah. I see that your heart has not been enlarged."

Manasseh

Another result of Hezekiah's constricted heart was that he fathered the most ungodly king of Judah's entire history—Manasseh. One reason Hezekiah cried so bitterly when God told him he would die was because Hezekiah had no heir. After God extended Hezekiah's life by fifteen years, Manasseh was conceived. This is a pivotal point in Judah's history. The nation plummeted, in part, because Hezekiah did not impart a love for God to his son Manasseh, and this precipitated the downfall of the nation.

Perhaps Hezekiah was too busy with kingdom business to commit himself vigorously to imparting a passion for godliness to his son. Whatever the reason, when Manasseh inherited the throne, he gave himself perversely to the lowest levels of idolatry, even to the point of sacrificing his own son in the fire. He practiced sorcery, consulted mediums, and filled Jerusalem with innocent blood (see II Kings 21:6; 24:4). It's amazing that a godly man like Hezekiah would raise such a rebel. However, Hezekiah's vision, unlike Abraham and David's, did not include future generations.

I want you to notice how God talks about Manasseh. Many years later, God is still outraged over Manasseh's wickedness. Notice what God says to Jeremiah a couple of generations later: **"Even if Moses and Samuel stood before Me, My mind would not be favorable toward this people. I will hand them over to trouble . . . because of Manasseh the son of Hezekiah, king of Judah, for what he did in Jerusalem"** (Jeremiah 15:1, 4). Even though the nation of Judah had a couple of spiritual awakenings after Manasseh, especially during the reign of Josiah, God had determined judgment on the nation. Even though the nation had repented, God could not dismiss Manasseh's abominations.

Who fathered Manasseh? The righteous king with the constricted heart.

The Bottom Line

Hezekiah represents the sincere believer who loves the Lord, but misses God's highest purposes. Herein is a fearful spiritual truth: it's possible to have a sincere heart to please God, and still be disqualified from God's best for our lives. When crisis and pressure come our way, let us humble ourselves in patience and love until our hearts are enlarged.

Perhaps your life has been hit recently with something traumatic. Allow your pain to sensitize you to the pain of others. You will weep over things you've never wept over before. You will feel yourself being stretched. Like Hezekiah, deliverance will come to you. But will you be any different when it comes? Let us not only seek deliverance, let us also renew ourselves to seek the highest of God's purposes—that we would be conformed to the image of His Son, who laid down His life as a ransom for many. May we allow our hearts to be enlarged, so God's purposes for this and future generations may be established through us.

Bob Sorge serves on the pastoral staff of Zion Fellowship in Canandaigua, NY. This article is condensed from a chapter in Bob's new book, *The Fire of Delayed Answers*. This book is available through your local Christian bookstore, or can be ordered by calling 1-716-394-7450.

THE MERCIES OF DAVID

by Bob Jones with Keith Davis

All Scripture references NAS unless otherwise indicated.

Recently Bob was given a series of visions, all related to one another, revealing a portion of the Lord's heart concerning this hour. These are issues necessary for us to hear the Lord's voice and prepare His permanent dwelling place during these last days.

In the first vision, Bob was shown a black porous mineral that looked similar to coal. In the vision, he began to crush this material into a powder and mix another substance with it, making what he determined to be mortar. In the second experience, on the day of Pentecost this year, Bob heard the Lord audibly stating that He was giving us *"the sure mercies of David, or the holy blessings of David."* In the third and final vision, Bob was shown a rainbow coming to the earth, which represented a covenant with the Lord. This rainbow was different from any other, however, in that it remained constant and did not dissipate. In

the vision, Bob began searching for the end of the rainbow to see what it contained. He discovered that while he was in the light of this rainbow, he experienced great love, peace and joy. Once he reached the end of the rainbow, instead of finding a pot of gold, he found the rainbow produced something of far greater value. The gold at the end of this rainbow was the *goals* that are the object of our faith—the fruit of the Spirit.

One Scripture that provides insight into these visions is Isaiah 55:3. It states, **"Incline your ear, and come to Me. Hear, and your soul shall live; and I will make an everlasting covenant with you—the sure mercies of David"** (NKJV). This outstanding covenant the Lord made with David can be found in II Samuel 7:8-29. In this passage, the Lord promised many things to David, yet we will see that particular parts of this covenant are important for this hour.

THE MERCIES OF DAVID

THE HEART OF DAVID

To understand these "sure mercies of David," we must understand some things about David himself. David was a man after God's own heart. In II Samuel 7 we find David searching his own heart after the Lord had given him victories over all his enemies and after his palace of cedar had been completed. He then finds it in his heart the desire to build a permanent dwelling place for the Lord. He inquires of his friend, Nathan who, speaking out of his own soul, tells David to do all that is in his heart, for the Lord is with him.

However, the Lord appears to Nathan and speaks a more sure word about the desire of David's heart. David's desire to build a permanent dwelling for the Lord pleased the Father, for it precipitated Him establishing an outstanding covenant with David. Through the covenant the Lord promised David victory over all his enemies, and an enduring house with a son sitting upon his throne. The Lord stated that a descendant would come from David whose kingdom would be established by the Lord. God would allow this man to build a house for His name sake, and His throne would be established forever. The Lord also stated that He would be a Father to this descendant of David and that he would be a son to the Lord. Of course, this was speaking of Jesus.

THE ONLY FOUNDATION

The description of this enduring house can be found in Isaiah 54:9-17. It states in verse 11 of chapter 54 that the Lord will set your stones in antimony. Antimony is a black mineral that was ground into powder during those days and used for a variety of purposes. When mixed with water, this powder could be used for such things as mascara and other cosmetic purposes.

However, when mixed with resin, the powder was used as a seal to set stones in jewelry or used as a mortar to set the foundation stones within a building. We believe the black porous stones that Bob crushed into powder, in his vision, were antimony.

It goes on to state in verse 11 that God will lay the foundations in sapphires. The sapphire represents the Lord's divine nature and His Holy character as seen in several Scriptures (see Exodus 24:10, Ezekiel 1:26, 10:1, Revelation 21:19). In both Ezekiel and Revelation we find descriptions of sapphire "under the Lord's feet," which signifies that the very foundation of all that the Lord does is built upon His divine nature and character.

In Acts 13:34-39 Paul revealed that the promise for the sure mercies of David was fulfilled through Christ when God raised Him from the dead. It is stated in Romans 1:4 that Jesus was raised from the dead by the Spirit of Holiness. Being raised from the dead by the spirit of Holiness proved that Jesus was indeed the Son of God, purchasing, for all who believe, the opportunity of becoming joint heirs with Him in the family of God. This is produced by our being the dwelling place of God.

Isaiah 54:17 states a profound promise to God's children:

> **No weapon that is formed against you shall prosper; and every tongue that accuses you in judgment you will condemn. *This is the heritage of the servants of the LORD.***

It is the heritage of the saints of God to receive the mercies of David, including protection from our enemies, the potential to become joint heirs, and the opportunity to become the habitation of God. This heritage was confirmed to David by the

THE MORNING STAR **29**

Spirit of Holiness (see Psalm 89:35), which was also intended to advance holiness in the hearts of those that would believe. From this we see the basic foundation of the house represented by the sapphire as the Divine Nature and Holy Character of God. It is only upon this foundation that successful Christian living or ministry can result.

OUR GOAL

In Bob's vision of the rainbow, it was revealed by God that the goal of our faith should be the fruit of the Spirit which are reflected in the Lord's divine nature. God wants us to have the fruit of the Spirit residing in us so that the power ministries necessary for the end time harvest do not destroy us. In this vision Bob was shown both sunlight and darkness, revealing that these times will produce simultaneously both cleansing and judgment. Just as with Israel, either blessings or cursings will be ours, depending on our choices (see Deuteronomy 28). Those who continue in the Son's light will increasingly become partakers of His divine nature bearing His fruit, while those who reject the Son's light will find themselves in despair and gross darkness.

Those who find themselves in this gross darkness must do as Paul stated in Acts 3:19:

Repent **therefore and** *return*, **that your sins may be wiped away, in order that times of refreshing may come from the presence of the Lord.**

Just as a citrus tree can only produce citrus fruit, because that is the life abiding within the tree, so it is with a Christian life. A Christian can only bear Godly fruit when the life of God is abiding in that person. Once that life finds its dwelling place in the heart of man, then the result will be the production of Godly fruit, just as the citrus tree by its very nature produces citrus fruit.

Luke 8:15 states, **"The seed in the good soil, these are the ones who have heard the word in an honest and good heart, and hold it fast, and bear fruit with perseverance."** The calling of the Christian is to be the permanent dwelling place of God, producing eternal fruit. This is done as we embrace the word of God, which is His seed, in an honest and good heart. As we receive His word and obey it, the Holy Spirit has greater freedom to bring forth His fruit in our lives.

As those who are in Christ, we have access into this covenant of the sure mercies of David. This covenant is sealed with us by God's Holy Spirit, the Spirit of Holiness. Paul in Ephesians 4:30 implored us to **"grieve not the holy Spirit of God, whereby ye are** *sealed unto the day of redemption*" (KJV). The mortar produced by mixing antimony with resin is symbolic of the Holy Spirit who seals us, as living stones, into the temple of God and into our rightful place within His body.

As Solomon did in II Chronicles 6:42, we should also ask the Lord to remember the promise that he made to his father David. When we put the Lord in remembrance of His promises, we are declaring that our faith is in Him and what He has spoken. Faith in God is what we need to be pleasing to Him. When our Lord was baptized in the Jordan River, the Scriptures declare that the heavens opened and the Holy Spirit descended in the form of a dove and remained on Him, the Father declaring, "This is My beloved *Son in Whom* I am well pleased." Some translators indicate that another rendering of this could read: "This is My Beloved Son in whom I am pleased to dwell."

With this seal of the Holy Spirit, Jesus was declared to be the Son of God and immediately He began to bear fruit for eternal purposes. So it is with us as we become the dwelling place of God. As the Holy Spirit tabernacles in us, we then begin to bear fruit and become partakers of His divine nature. The basis for this is the sure mercies of David, the promise that God has given us victory over our enemies, the opportunity for sonship and the right to be His dwelling place. All of this was purchased for us through the blood of Christ, who was the Son that God promised would come from David's lineage. We partake of this covenant through hearing the Lord's voice and placing our faith in His Word.

Second Peter 1:3-4 outlines this principle:

> **Seeing that His divine power has granted to us everything pertaining to life and godliness,** *through the true knowledge of Him* **who called us by His own glory and excellence.**
>
> **For by these He has granted to us His precious and magnificent promises, in order that by them you might become partakers of the divine nature.**

Only through the true knowledge of Christ revealed to us through the Spirit of Truth can we obtain life and godliness, resulting in the sharing of His divine nature. This knowledge comes as we continue abiding in Him who is our Life and giving heed to His voice.

From these visions it seems that the prophetic message for this hour clearly reminds us to be tender as the Spirit of Truth brings us into greater knowledge of God and His purposes. We should not harden our hearts as we hear the Lord's voice through His messengers. God wants to remove the man-made traditions that have made His word ineffectual (see Mark 7). It is through the true knowledge of Christ that we are sanctified (see John 17:17). As Isaiah 55:3 declares, **"Incline your ear, and come to Me. Hear, and your soul shall live; and I will make an everlasting covenant with you—***the sure mercies of David***"** (NKJV). ∎

Bob Jones is one of the most uniquely gifted man in the prophetic of our time. He has personally ministered to thousands of today's leaders. In preparing the body of Christ, Bob continues to lay "power lines" between the leaders of the church to repair the breech and draw the church into unity with one purpose. Bob has traveled abroad ministering in churches and conferences, and continues to "build bridges" with the leadership of the end-time church. His focus is to encourage the end-time church to come to a place of relationship with the magnificent "Abba" Father, resulting in the restoration and reconciliation which will exemplify the Father's true Love . . . and Power!

False Prophets & False Prophecy

by Rick Joyner

All Scripture references NAS unless otherwise indicated.

When the Lord was asked by His disciples what the signs of the end of the age would be, He began His answer with, **"See to it that no one misleads you" (Matthew 24:4)**. While then listing a number of events in the perilous times at the end, He included, **"For false Christs and false prophets will arise and will show great signs and wonders, so as to mislead, if possible, even the elect" (verse 24)**. As we get closer to the end of this age it is therefore increasingly important for us to be able to recognize these false Christs and false prophets.

Discernment Principle Number One

The most important principle for discerning the false is to know the true. The better we know someone, the less likely we are to be fooled by someone who tries to disguise themselves as that person. The better we know the Lord, the less likely we are to be fooled by any spirit that claims to be Him. Likewise, the better we know true prophecy, the less likely we are to be deceived by the false.

The warning about "false Christs" is not just a warning about those who claim to be Christ. The word for "Christ" in this text could also be translated, "anointed." Because the Scriptures are so clear about the nature of the Lord's return, if anyone claimed to be Him we would immediately know that he was an imposter. Therefore the warning is probably meant to be much more general, warning us that many will come claiming to be "anointed" of God and be imposters.

This is not to disregard the fact that the Lord was also warning us of those who would claim to be *the Christ*. Many non-Christians and pseudo-Christians have been, and will continue to be, carried away with false

Christs. However, those who know the true Christ will not be fooled by false Christs. False prophets will obviously be a much greater danger to the true church than false Christs.

I have personally watched a number of churches and ministries devastated by false prophets, or false prophecies. Much of the church today is becoming increasingly subject to false prophecy. Why? For basically the same reason those who do not know the true Christ are subject to believing in false ones. Those who do not know true prophecy will be easily fooled by the false.

Some of the more glaring examples of this have come through the false prophecies which set a date for the Lord's return. It is most sobering to watch so much of the church get caught up with these prophecies, which are in clear contradiction to the Scripture which states that "no man knows the time." It should also be enlightening to see how those churches and movements which are so easily captured by these false prophecies are mostly those which reject the gift of prophecy as being for the church today.

A recent example of this was when so much of the church was swept up with the "88 Reasons Why the Lord Will Return in 1988." Every one of the prophetic people I knew at that time, and the movements that were seeking to grow in prophetic ministry, easily discerned this as a spurious prophecy. It was also alarming that so many who were so distracted by this did not ever seem to confess their mistake after it had become so obvious, or even examine how this happened to them. Remarkably, many of these simply expressed an increased disdain for the gift of prophecy.

If Paul the apostle admitted to having been "foiled by Satan," it can happen to any of us. Those who think that it cannot happen to them is probably in the greatest danger of having it happen to them. Our response to this should not be to reject prophecy, which is such a central theme of Scripture, and has been a primary way that the Lord has related to His people from the beginning. Our response must be to increase our resolve to know the true so we can quickly discern the false.

It is also biblical wisdom to "not be ignorant of Satan's schemes." Therefore it is right that we examine ways that either we or others have been fooled in the past. So, to sum up Principle Number One, we need to know the true, but admit our need for God's grace and wisdom, being willing to honestly admit our mistakes.

Discernment Principle Number Two

One can be a true believer but still be a false prophet, or give false prophecies. The Lord Jesus Himself confirmed this in Matthew 24:4-5: **"And Jesus answered and said to them, 'See to it that no one misleads you. For many will come in My name, saying, "I am the Christ," and will mislead many.' "** The Lord did not say that these would come and say that *they* were the Christ, but that they would come saying that He, Jesus, was the Christ, and yet they would still mislead many. History has testified to the truth of this, as some of the most destructive false prophets stated that Jesus was the Christ, and yet deceived many. How can this happen?

False prophets and false prophecies are founded upon deception. The most effective guise of the enemy is to come as "an angel of light," or "a messenger of truth." Just because a prophecy has some truth in it does not make it genuine. Unfortunately, Satan knows the Bible better than most Christians. He is so clever at perverting its message that he even tried it on Jesus, Who is the Word Himself. The most effective false prophets who have and will continue to be used by Satan are usually very skillful in the use of Scripture. Just knowing Scripture, and being able to bludgeon others into submission with it, does not make one a true messenger. We must ask if they are "rightly dividing the word of truth."

Who is the authority on whether the word is being rightly divided? The One who wrote the book. Doesn't that leave a lot of room for subjectivity in our discernment? Yes. It utterly compels us to be dependent on the Holy Spirit. If we do not know the Lord's voice we will continually be fooled by all of the other voices in the world. There will never be a principle so full of wisdom that it will be a substitute for knowing the Lord's voice for ourselves.

This does mean that subjectivity exists in discernment, but subjectivity not only exists—it is essential for discernment of truth. No one will be saved because they know someone else who is. We are not lovers of truth just because we know someone who knows the truth. The Lord must become our personal Savior, our personal Lord, and truth must be personal if we are really going to know it. For this reason the Bible was meant to be relatively subjective in its interpretation. This was not to promote private interpretations, but to require each of us to be seekers of the Lord and His truth ourselves. We will not keep from being deceived just because we know someone who knows the Bible. Everyone of us must know the Spirit of Truth.

Many systems of hermeneutics have been devised by men seeking to remove subjectivity from biblical interpretation. Many of these are excellent helps, but regardless of how good our hermeneutics are, if we do not know and follow the Spirit of Truth we will be increasingly subject to deception in the coming times. Many hermeneutical principles developed by men are actually an attempt to remove our need for the Holy Spirit, regardless of how much they give lip service to needing Him. This will only lead to deception, not prevent it.

To sum up Discernment Principle Number Two, we will not keep from being deceived without the Holy Spirit. The better we know Him, and the closer we remain to Him, the safer we will be. This is true with doctrine and

with prophecy. Understanding these foundational principles, the following are general deceptions that open people up to false prophets, or false prophecies.

Deception Number One: Deception usually begins with allowing any truth, even a biblical truth, to eclipse the centrality of Christ.

Christ is the ultimate purpose of God. As Mike Bickle once said, "If we do not keep our attention focused on the ultimate purpose of God, we will be distracted by the lesser purposes of God." Our purpose is to grow up into Christ, to become like Him, and to do the works that He did. Those who go into extremes, or become eccentric (which means to be "off center"), do so because they lose their focus on the ultimate purpose of God. As Ephesians 1:9-10 states:

> **He made known to us the mystery of His will, according to His kind intention which He purposed in Him**
>
> **with a view to an administration suitable to the fulness of the times, that is, the summing up of all things in Christ, things in the heavens and things upon the earth.**

Colossians 1:28-29 states:

> **And we proclaim Him, admonishing every man and teaching every man with all wisdom, that we may present every man complete in Christ.**
>
> **And for this purpose also I labor, striving according to His power, which mightily works within me.**

The central purpose of the church is to reveal Jesus. We do that by becoming like Him. The apostolic commission was not to just teach truths, but to labor until Christ was formed in His church. Only when He is formed in us can we do the works that He did. Only when we abide in the One who is the Truth will we cease to be subject to the father of lies. We must never let any doctrine or emphasis eclipse our simple devotion to being close to Him and becoming like Him. As the apostle prayed:

But I am afraid, lest as the serpent deceived Eve by his craftiness, your minds should be led astray from the simplicity and purity of devotion to Christ (II Corinthians 11:3).

The ultimate goal of the Father is to have all things summed up in His Son. Truths, the church, the ministry, even worship, can become idols if we allow them to take Jesus' rightful place as the central focus of our devotion.

Deception Number Two: Those who become too sympathetic to the interests of men can be used to speak for the evil one.

But He turned and said to Peter, "Get behind Me, Satan! You are a stumbling block to Me; for you are not setting your mind on God's interests, but man's" (Matthew 16:23).

This is usually caused by *unsanctified mercy*, which is having mercy for the things that God is judging. This is usually the result of getting the two great commandments out of order, which causes us to love the people more than we love the Lord. We are commanded to love men, but we must not let our hearts be captured by the interests of men. As James warned: **"You adulteresses, do you not know that friendship with the world is hostility toward God? Therefore whoever wishes to be a friend of the world makes himself an enemy of God" (James 4:4).**

The ways of fallen men are contrary to the ways of the Lord. What men purpose to do is often the opposite of what the Lord purposes to do. To the degree that we are subject to the influences of fallen men we will be found doing that which is contrary to God. The Lord Jesus said, **"And He said to them [the Pharisees], 'You are those who justify yourselves in the sight of men, but God knows your hearts; for that which is highly** esteemed among men is detestable in the sight of God' " (Luke 16:15).** The reverse is also true; the things that are highly esteemed by God are usually detestable in the sight of men. *Someone* is going to detest what we are doing. Who do we want it to be, God or men? That is why Paul said: **"If I were still trying to please men, I would not be a bondservant of Christ" (Galatians 1:10).**

The Lord Jesus also said, **"Woe to you when all men speak well of you, for in the same way their fathers used to treat the false prophets" (Luke 6:26).** We must be to at least some degree deceived when we are encouraged by the approval of fallen men. Whenever the gospel has been preached in its true purity and power it has brought the most vehement persecution from men. We should actually be much more concerned if we are not being persecuted.

Jeremiah made a most sobering observation: **"The prophets prophesy falsely, and the priests rule on their own authority; and My people love it so! But what will you do at the end of it?" (Jeremiah 5:31).** The people will actually love false prophecy, and if we are subject to the fear of man we will end up prophesying falsely in order to please them.

Deception Number Three: Deception will result when self-seeking or selfish ambition enter a ministry.

When we have beheld the glory of Jesus, His nature, His power, His sacrifice, to use the ministry that we do in His name for selfish reasons must be considered the very definition of profanity. As the Lord declared in John 7:18: **"He who speaks from himself seeks his own glory; but He who is seeking the glory of the one who sent Him, He is true, and there is no unrighteousness in Him."**

As He stated in John 5:44: **"How can you believe, when you receive glory from one another, and you do not seek the glory that is from the one and only God."** Receiving glory from men is the most detrimental factor that destroys true faith, and it can be a primary factor in having us speak for the sake of men rather than for God, which is a root of false prophetic ministry.

Deception Number Four: An unholy familiarity with God can lead to deception about Him.

True prophetic ministry must have a proper balance between friendship with the Lord, and the fear of God. John was intimate with the Lord, but Judas was familiar. There is a difference between these two. Even though John was close enough to the Lord to lay his head on His breast, when he saw the resurrected Christ during his revelation, he fell to the ground like a dead man. That is what Paul meant when he exhorted the church to know both **"the kindness and the severity of God (Romans 11:22)."**

Amos 3:7 states: **"Surely the Lord GOD does nothing unless He reveals His secret counsel to His servants the prophets."** The Lord does this because the prophets are His friends and He does not want to do anything without sharing it with them. That is fundamentally the essence of true prophetic ministry, simply being so close to God that He does not want to do anything without sharing it with you. Even so, Psalm 25:14 adds: **"The secret of the LORD is for those who fear Him."** Wisdom is to seek to be as close to Him as we possibly can be, while at the same time remembering who He is and who we are. Anyone who does not fear the Lord has not seen Him as He is.

One characteristic that is evident in the lives of all true prophets is the pure and holy fear of the Lord. It is a fearful thing to presume to speak in the name of the Lord when He has not spoken. What could be more of a delusion than to presume to put words into the mouth of Almighty God? Beware of any messenger who does not display this holy fear of the Lord.

Deception Number Five: Beware of those who do not walk in what they preach.

Thus says the LORD of hosts, **"Do not listen to the words of the prophets who are prophesying to you. They are leading you into futility; they speak a vision of their own imagination, not from the mouth of the LORD.**

"They keep saying to those who despise Me, 'The LORD has said, "You will have peace" '; and as for everyone who walks in the stubbornness of his own heart, they say, 'Calamity will not come upon you.'

"But who has stood in the council of the LORD, that he should see and hear His word? Who has given heed to His word and listened?" (Jeremiah 23:16-18).

A key element for anyone who would walk in a true prophetic ministry is faithfulness to their own message: *"who has stood in the council of the Lord?"* Beware of those who do not walk in what they preach. This is not to say that we cannot make mistakes, or at times fall short of what we are proclaim. As James said, **"We all stumble in many ways."** However, we can discern between those who are sincerely seeking to obey and live uprightly before the Lord, and those who preach His words but do not do them.

Deception Number Six: Beware of those who steal words from others.

"Is not My word like fire?" declares the LORD, **"and like a hammer which shatters a rock?**

"Therefore behold, I am against the prophets," declares the LORD, *"who steal My words from each other"* (Jeremiah 23:29-30).

There are elements to delivering a prophetic word that require the prophet to be in unity with his message. That is why the Lord told Ezekiel to eat the word himself before he went to speak to the people (see Ezekiel 3:1-4). A prophet is required to digest the word himself before he is qualified to speak it.

The reason that a true prophecy comes with the power to be "like fire," or "like a hammer which shatters a rock," is that it must come from the depths of the messenger himself with full conviction. Living waters can only come out of "the innermost being." If we are going to be prophetic we must have our own well, our own relationship to the Lord, and our own revelation. Prophets are not parrots.

This does not mean that we can never preach or prophesy what someone else has previously said. Every time we preach from the Scriptures we do this. It does mean that it must be more than a mental concept to us. It is not by believing in our minds, but in our hearts, that it results in righteousness (see Romans 10:10).

Deception Number Seven: Prophesying prejudices is the source of many false prophecies.

Those who allow prejudices to influence what they attach "thus saith the Lord" to will become false. Prejudices are strongholds that can be cultural, religious, racial, the result of unhealed wounds, or character flaws. For anyone who feels called to the prophetic ministry, or who is sometimes used in prophetic gifts, we must heed the exhortation, **"Watch over your heart with all diligence, for from it flow the springs of life" (Proverbs 4:23).** The following are a few of the more common prejudices that can wrongly influence prophecy:

Pet Doctrines. The Lord does not give prophecies to verify doctrines—He gave the Bible for that. Prophecy was used to write Scripture, but now that the Canon is complete, prophecy is not used to verify or establish doctrine. It may be used to illuminate specific applications of Scripture, such as the revelation that Peter had that led him to preach the gospel to the Gentiles, but that is not the same as using it to establish a doctrine. Beware of using prophecy to verify doctrines, especially those which are ambiguous or obscure.

Bitterness or resentment can also influence our message. This is why the priests in the Old Testament could not have scabs. Scabs are unhealed wounds. Unhealed wounds can be a destructive element in any ministry. If we have unhealed wounds it is because we have not taken them to the cross and applied the balm of forgiveness. Anyone who is walking in unforgiveness can be easily subjected to deception.

Rejection is another problem that can turn a true prophet into a false one. Prophets are often rejected, and if we are going to be prophetic that is something that we must learn to live with, without becoming reactionary or bitter. The Lord often allows His prophets to be rejected to deliver them from the fear of man. But if we still have feelings of rejection, or continue to be overly sensitive to rejection, we know that we have an unhealed wound that can affect our perception.

Rebellion is another stronghold that can lead to false prophecy. Rebellion is rooted either in rejection, self-will, or both. This can be deadly to the prophetic ministry. As Samuel warned King Saul, **"rebellion is as the sin of witchcraft" (I Samuel 15:23).** Witchcraft is counterfeit spiritual authority that is exactly contrary to the prophetic ministry. There can be a fine line between divination and revelation, and if rebellion is in our heart we can easily be lead into crossing that line.

The "party spirit," or sectarianism, can also lead to false prophecy. When we derive our recognition from a single organization there will be pressure to prophesy the "party line." This can make it very difficult not to compromise prophetic integrity.

Of course, these strongholds can pervert any ministry, not just the prophetic. Neither is this meant to imply that we must be perfect before the Lord can use us. But we must esteem the word of the Lord so that we would never let our own opinions or flaws influence what we say in His great name. The more respect we have for this the more spiritual authority and revelation He can trust us with.

Deception Number Eight: Presuming more authority than the Lord has given to us can lead to our becoming false.

Even if the Lord gives us a revelation, that does not necessarily give us authority to dictate policy, or to compel others to take action on it. If we go beyond the sphere of authority appointed to us we are false in what we have presumed.

In the Old Testament, prophets were often called "watchmen" because they were spiritually stationed on "the walls of Jerusalem." From that position they would be the first to see someone coming. It was the watchman's job to distinguish between friend or foe and to convey what he discerned to the elders who sat in the gates. However, it was not the watchman's job to determine what action should then be taken. It was the elder who made this judgment. It was also the elder's responsibility to determine if someone was to be let in or kept out of the city, or to sound the alarm to mobilize troops.

Once the prophet gave his report, it was no longer his place to see that it was acted upon in what he thought was a proper manner. That was the job of the authorities which had been established for that purpose. The Lord has also established pastors and elders in the church for that purpose. After we receive a prophetic revelation and it is given to those in authority, we must leave it in their hands to take action on, or not to.

Many prophetic people fall into the trap of believing that because they were shown something, they have the responsibility to see it brought to pass. From that they will assume the authority to carry it out. This brings many unnecessary conflicts to congregations and ministries. Paul talked about how careful he was to stay within the realm of authority that had been appointed to him (see II Corinthians 10:12-14). Here he was speaking geographically, but it is just as true spiritually. Just as a

policeman in New York does not have authority in Paris, and could get into serious trouble trying to exercise it there, we too often get into trouble because we try to exercise authority where it has not been given to us.

Paul also said to the Corinthians, **"If to others I am not an apostle, at least I am to you"** (I Corinthians 9:2). By this Paul was acknowledging that he was not an apostle to the whole church, but only to those that he had been used in an apostolic way. He was an apostle to the Gentiles. When he tried to go to the Jews he got into trouble. Peter was an apostle to the Jews. When he tried to go to the Gentiles, he got into trouble and Paul had to rebuke him.

When Paul went to Jerusalem he was acknowledged as being an apostle to the Gentiles, but he was not given apostolic authority in the church in Jerusalem. He could not dictate policy there like he could have in the churches that he had been used to raise up. In Jerusalem he was just a visiting missionary, honored and esteemed, but not followed.

Many prophetic people fall into the trap of feeling the responsibility to tear down anything that they do not believe is from the Lord. However, we only have authority to tear down that which we have been used to raise up. Paul warned the church in Corinth that he had authority to tear down as well as build up because he had been used to build the church there. It would have been presumption for Paul to try to tear down the work that he did not like in Jerusalem, or anywhere else that he had not been the builder. He was the father of the church in Corinth. Would any responsible father let just anyone come in and start bringing correction, or dictating policy, to his family? I would not let anyone bring correction to a work that I had responsibility for unless they had also been used in the building of it. If you are a responsible leader of a church or work, and someone claims to be sent to bring correction or set things in order, and they have not been a part of the building, do not feel that you will be missing God to throw them out.

True spiritual authority is built on love and trust. We will not have spiritual authority with anyone that we do not love, or who do not trust us. Trust is earned by love and service. If a person comes to me with a corrective word about what to do in the nursery, but has never been willing to work in the nursery, I will not even bother to listen to him. Like most pastors, I get piles of prophecies from people who try to dictate policy in our ministry, and many of them I do not even know! Such misuses of "prophecy" make it understandable why so many pastors come to despise prophecy. Such misuses have caused so many problems that any pastor who has an openness to prophecy at all is demonstrating extraordinary grace, and should certainly be appreciated.

Many who claim to be watchmen do not have the proper trust relationship with the elders of the church, and they therefore often try to usurp the authority of the elders. If we are called as watchmen, we must allow the Lord to establish our authority with those who have authority, and not strive to gain influence ourselves. As a pastor, whenever someone strives to gain my recognition I become that much more wary of them. The striving itself reveals a lack of maturity that should make us cautious.

Deception Number Nine: Beware of any word that does not come in the demonstration of the fruit of the Spirit, regardless of how much power is demonstrated. As James explained:

> **Not many of you should presume to be teachers, my brothers, because you know that we who teach will be judged more strictly.**
>
> **We all stumble in many ways. If anyone is never at fault in what he says, he is a perfect man, able to keep his whole body in check.**

> **When we put bits into the mouths of horses to make them obey us, we can turn the whole animal.**
>
> **Or take ships as an example. Although they are so large and are driven by strong winds, they are steered by a very small rudder wherever the pilot wants to go.**
>
> **Likewise the tongue is a small part of the body, but it makes great boasts. Consider what a great forest is set on fire by a small spark.**
>
> **The tongue also is a fire, a world of evil among the parts of the body. It corrupts the whole person, sets the whole course of his life on fire, and is itself set on fire by hell.**
>
> **All kinds of animals, birds, reptiles and creatures of the sea are being tamed and have been tamed by man,**
>
> **but no man can tame the tongue. It is a restless evil, full of deadly poison.**
>
> **With the tongue we praise our Lord and Father, and with it we curse men, who have been made in God's likeness.**
>
> **Out of the same mouth come praise and cursing. My brothers, this should not be.**
>
> **Can both fresh water and salt water flow from the same spring?**
>
> **My brothers, can a fig tree bear olives, or a grapevine bear figs? Neither can a salt spring produce fresh water.**
>
> **Who is wise and understanding among you? Let him show it by his good life, by deeds done in the humility that comes from wisdom.**
>
> **But if you harbor bitter envy and selfish ambition in your hearts, do not boast about it or deny the truth.**
>
> **Such "wisdom" does not come down from heaven but is earthly, unspiritual, of the devil.**

For where you have envy and selfish ambition, there you find disorder and every evil practice.

But the wisdom that comes from heaven is first of all pure; then peaceloving, considerate, submissive, full of mercy and good fruit, impartial and sincere.

Peacemakers who sow in peace raise a harvest of righteousness (James 3:1-18).

Moses was denied the blessing of leading the people into their Promised Land because the Lord told him to speak to the rock to bring forth water, but he struck the rock in anger. As a prophet he represented the Lord as angry when He was not, and it cost him dearly. It is easy to understand how Moses was frustrated, but we must never convey our own feelings as being the way the Lord feels. Many prophetic people have disqualified themselves from higher realms of authority by representing the Lord improperly this way.

It is a serious delusion to think that because God occasionally uses us to speak through that He thinks just like we do, or that our feelings are His feelings. We must be careful to distinguish our own feelings from that which is coming by the anointing. This is not easy to do, even for mature prophets. It is therefore good to never trust "revelations" that come concerning those that we have personally been rejected by. Whenever we are rejected or attacked by someone, they should go on our prayer list. We should pray for them and their ministry until we have such an investment in them that we deeply care for their welfare. If bitterness gets a root in us it will defile us and many more.

Elijah prayed for the judgments of the Lord to come on the people, but it was not out of his own wrath. God's wrath is not like man's wrath. Neither is His jealousy like man's, which is self-centered. We must always be careful not to represent our anger as being the Lord's, or we can end up like Moses and never enter the fulness of what we have been called to. Whenever we think we have a word of correction, or judgment, for another ministry or person, we should ask ourselves two important questions: Do we love them? Has God given us authority with them? Has the bridge of trust been built so they could even be expected to receive what we think we should share with them?

Deception Number Ten: We will be deceived if we spend more time studying deception than we do studying the truth.

The Lord warned the church of Thyatira about "knowing the deep things of Satan" (see Revelation 2:24). We will be changed into the image of what we are beholding (see II Corinthians 3:18). If we spend too much time looking for or at the enemy, we will be changed into his image. This is why many cult watchers and heresy hunters often become mean-spirited. Some are then used to do more damage to the church than many false teachers or false prophets ever could.

We must be vigilant and able to quickly recognize the enemy, but not be too quick to call someone the enemy until we are sure of what we see. A friend of mine who was a close associate of Jack Coe, one of the greatest of the healing evangelists, told me how he died quickly and unexpectedly at the age of just 39 after publicly referring to Kathryn Kuhlman as a witch. Years later, Kuhlman died quickly and unexpectedly after publicly calling Bob Mumford a false teacher. Were these the judgments of God? I believe both of these died because of the mercy of the Lord, to keep them from crossing the line to becoming a stumbling block, something the Lord Himself warned should be the last thing we ever want to become. (I believe that I have shared the above with the permission of the Lord, and am not in any way trying to demean the great ministries of these two. As I also believe that they are a part of the "great company of witnesses"; I am also sure that they too want the church to know the truth of this.)

Deception Number Eleven: Thinking that we alone have the truth, or that we alone are left faithful, is a profound delusion.

Elijah was one of the greatest prophets who ever lived, yet he was deceived into thinking that he alone was left of the prophets faithful to the Lord. After making this statement the Lord told him to prepare for his own departure. When this deception gets into our soul, our time of usefulness on this earth is probably over. After a life of faithfulness and doing exploits in the name of the Lord, why have so many great men and women of God turned into false prophets, false teachers, or false shepherds? In many of these cases it was the result of this delusion, that they alone had the truth, or that they alone were faithful.

Deception Number Twelve: Sin.

But encourage one another day after day, as long as it is still called "Today," lest any one of you be hardened by *the deceitfulness of sin* (Hebrews 3:13).

Because prophets are called to be "eyes," or to see for the body, the enemy usually concentrates his attack on them through their eyes. Therefore pornography or other forms of lust are serious traps for them. If we are going to function as the eye of the body we must be careful how we use our eyes. In this, Job showed great wisdom when he said, **"I have made a covenant with my eyes; how then could I gaze at a virgin?" (Job 31:1).** Job made a covenant with his eyes not to look upon something that would cause him to stumble. If our eye is single, upon the Lord, our whole body will be full of light. If we use our eyes to look upon that which promotes lust or other sin, darkness will enter out soul. From that darkness deception will come.

Deception Number Thirteen: It is a deception for New Covenant prophets to type themselves after Old Covenant prophets.

The spiritual gifts of New Testament prophets are basically the same as in the Old Testament, but the function of the New Testament prophet is very different. Many

Anonymous:

★ Warren Wiersbe said: "We have too many people who have plenty of medals and no scars." I wonder if he was talking about an army or the church?

★ The Holy Spirit guarantees the finished product, not our dignity along the way.

★ While it's true God never changes, He never stands still, either.

★ A true servant will value another's time above their own.

think of prophets as harsh and always looking for what is wrong with people. That was often the nature of the Old Covenant prophet, because he was under law and therefore had to represent the severity of the law. However, the New Testament prophet is under the covenant of grace and truth, and must represent that covenant. The Lord did not come to condemn us, but to save us by laying down His own life for us. That should be the nature of anyone who is called to speak for Him in this age of grace and truth. Truth without grace will at best be only half the message.

Another major difference between the prophets under the different covenants is that the Old Covenant prophets often stood alone, but the New Covenant prophets are but one of a team of ministries given for the equipping of the church. Therefore the New Covenant prophet must be properly related to the rest of the ministry team that God has given to His church. Just as the nature and function of a hand cannot be fully understood without an understanding of the arm and the rest of the body to which it is connected, the New Covenant prophetic ministry cannot be fully understood without an understanding, and proper fitting with, the other equipping ministries listed in Ephesians 4, the apostles, evangelists, pastors and teachers.

Another serious deception can enter into a ministry when a young, immature prophet tries to live under the Old Covenant mandate for prophets given in Deuteronomy 18:18-22:

"I will raise up a prophet from among their countrymen like you, and I will put My words in his mouth, and he shall speak to them all that I command him.

"And it shall come about that whoever will not listen to My words which he shall speak in My name, I Myself will require it of him.

"But the prophet who shall speak a word presumptuously in My name which I have not commanded him to speak, or which he shall speak in the name of other gods, that prophet shall die.

"And you may say in your heart, 'How shall we know the word which the LORD has not spoken?'

"When a prophet speaks in the name of the LORD, if the thing does not come about or come true, that is the thing which the LORD has not spoken. The prophet has spoken it presumptuously; you shall not be afraid of him."

This was the standard under the law, and was a reflection of the standard under which everyone lived at that time. Under that covenant anyone who failed in any point of the law was under condemnation to the whole law. However, we cannot put the New Testament prophet under the law without putting the rest of the body under the Law as well.

What pastor or teacher could live under a yoke that removed him from his ministry if he made just one mistake? When young, struggling prophetic ministries try to comply with this Old Covenant mandate it will seriously distort their development, and their character. This yoke makes it impossible for them to acknowledge and learn from their mistakes.

This does not mean that we can compromise the high standards required of one who would speak for the Lord. Mistakes must be addressed and the reasons for them found. A mature, commissioned prophet should not miss. But this is not just for prophets; every ministry represents the Lord and should live under the highest standards, always acknowledging and seeking to understand their mistakes. Even so, we must not make the standards impossible by exceeding those required by the New Covenant. No prophet is infallible, which is why New Covenant prophecy must be judged. There are even cases where Old Covenant prophets missed a prediction or prophecy, but were still acknowledged as prophets by the Lord (Jonah, Isaiah and Elijah all made statements that were not true or did not come to pass). Because anyone can make a mistake, it keeps the responsibility on the whole church to know the Lord's voice.

Deception Number Fourteen: The deception that assumes that prophets are for some reason not required to use proper biblical protocol or procedure.

The most common place where improper procedure can lead to deception is in bringing correction. The prophets under the Old Covenant were used mostly to bring correction to the Lord's people, but this is not the case in the New Testament. In the New Testament this duty was assumed by the apostles and elders. This does not mean that a prophet cannot be used to bring correction, but it is no longer a primary responsibility. And when prophets are used this way, they must comply with the New Covenant procedure for correction given in Matthew 18 and Galatians 6:1. Anyone who tries to bring correction to someone else publicly who has not first been to them privately, and then with another witness, is at best out of order. At worst, they are a stumbling block.

Deception Number Fifteen: This is the presumption that prophecy must be specific or spectacular.

Generally, prophetic words are general. For example, the Lord could have been much more specific with His prophecies in the Scriptures. He could have told of the emergence of America, the dates and places that the world wars would start, or any other great events in history in much more detail than He chose to. Prophecy is seldom given to convince someone that the Lord exists, or to testify that we are His messengers. It is given for revealing His strategic will, and for awakening the church to her need to prepare for coming events or conditions. The Lord also usually wants prophecy to be general

enough to require those who receive it to both know His voice, and still have to walk in faith and wisdom. We have learned that the more specific and spectacular a prophecy is, the more difficult the task will be. Many have turned a good prophecy into a false one by trying to go beyond what they were given in order to make it more spectacular.

Paul Cain once said that he believed almost every heresy was the result of men trying to carry to logical conclusions that which God has only revealed in part. I think history corroborates that statement. It is often the Lord's intent for prophecy to be incomplete in order to keep the recipient seeking Him.

Understanding the Wizard Spirit

The "wizard" will be one of the primary forms that false prophets will come in last days when trying to infiltrate the body of Christ. They will usually have a clean, professional appearance, and will often try to establish their credibility by "prophesying" information that they know in the natural. One of their chief weapons flattery. Their chief deception will be to divert us from the purposes that the Lord has for us by prophesying to us things that are either greater, or seem more glamorous, than what the He has given us to do. Please consider the following Scriptures:

> They speak falsehood to one another; *with flattering lips* and with a double heart they speak.
> May the LORD cut off all *flattering lips*, the tongue that *speaks great things* (Psalm 12:2-3).

> For we never came with flattering speech, as you know, nor with a pretext for greed—God is witness—
> nor did we seek glory from men, either from you or from others, even though as apostles of Christ we might

have asserted our authority (I Thessalonians 2:5-6).

A flattering mouth works ruin (Proverbs 26:28).

For there will no longer be any false vision or flattering divination within the house of Israel...

Then the word of the LORD came to me saying,

"Son of man, prophesy against the prophets of Israel who prophesy, and say to those who prophesy from their own inspiration, 'Listen to the word of the LORD!

'Thus says the Lord GOD, "Woe to the foolish prophets who are following their own spirit and have seen nothing.

"O Israel, your prophets have been like foxes among ruins.

"You have not gone up into the breaches, nor did you build the wall around the house of Israel to stand in the battle on the day of the LORD.

"They see falsehood and lying divination who are saying, 'The LORD declares,' when the LORD has not sent them; yet they hope for the fulfillment of their word.

"Did you not see a false vision and speak a lying divination when you said, 'The LORD declares,' but it is not I who have spoken?'''"

Therefore, thus says the Lord GOD, "Because you have spoken falsehood and seen a lie, therefore behold, I am against you," declares the Lord GOD.

"So My hand will be against the prophets who see false visions and utter lying divinations. They will have no place in the council of My people, nor will they be written down in the register of the house of Israel, nor will they enter the land of Israel, that you may know that I am the Lord GOD.

"It is definitely because they have misled My people by saying, 'Peace!' when there is no peace. And when anyone builds a wall, behold, they plaster it over with whitewash" (Ezekiel 12:24-13:10).

One of the responsibilities of biblical prophets was to confront and expose false prophets. Those who are going to be true must face up to this responsibility. This is one of the most uncomfortable of tasks for the prophets because it will probably make them appear to be self-serving, or even self-righteous. Even so, if we are going to be real we must esteem the interests of the Lord, and the welfare of His people above how we appear.

Summary

Every one of the gifts and ministries that the Holy Spirit has given to the church is essential if we are to be properly equipped to do His will. Just as the Lord promised, at the end of the age prophecies, visions and dreams are being poured out (see Acts 2:17). These are being given because we will need them for accomplishing our last day mandate. As the prophetic gifts entrusted to the church become increasingly powerful, we must become even more careful not to misuse them. To speak in the name of the Lord is the greatest responsibility that will ever be entrusted to us. Those who are trusted with the greatest prophetic authority will be those who are the most trustworthy. It is imperative that if we are going to be used prophetically we remain humble and correctable, and increasingly sensitive and dependent on the Spirit of Truth. ■

Revival

by
Joni Ames

Not by power, not by might
But by My Spirit now
And you shall know Me even more
If, just to Me, you bow

Look for Me and seek My face
And look inside at you
And let me do My work inside
To you that I must do

Seek not the face of angry men
Nor of their worldly power
For I'll consume both it and them
Inside this final hour

For as I placed the stars above
And called this world to be
Revival only comes and stays
By what is done through Me

Hold not to things done in the past
Nor deeds men do today
But seek My face, and only Me
In all, give thanks and pray

I must revive your inner man
For you to do My Will
And you must truly feed on Me
Until you get your fill

For then and only then shall come
Forth rivers made of Me
And then and only then shall come
The power to set men free

continued . . .

For only I have what you need
　And only I can give
　　That resurrection power to man
　　　To be revived and live

Then as you walk, My power shall fall
　And many be set free
　　But you must let My Words of Life
　　　Extend through you from Me

Be strong in Me, allow My Love
　To tend My Sheep through you
　　Then greater things shall come to be
　　　Than man, alone, can do!

You must know Me to truly be
　My tools that I work through
　　And be My hands and feet and heart—
　　　That's what you have to do!

Reside in Me and I shall come
　And I'll reside in you
　　And you will be new vessels, pure,
　　　That I may then work through

Behold, attention draweth nigh
　To all called by My Name
　　Do not allow yourselves to be
　　　A people called to shame

Return to Me and only Me
　And let Me guide the way
　　Let true revival start with you
　　　And be revived today!

The Power of Your Musical Gift

BY DON POTTER

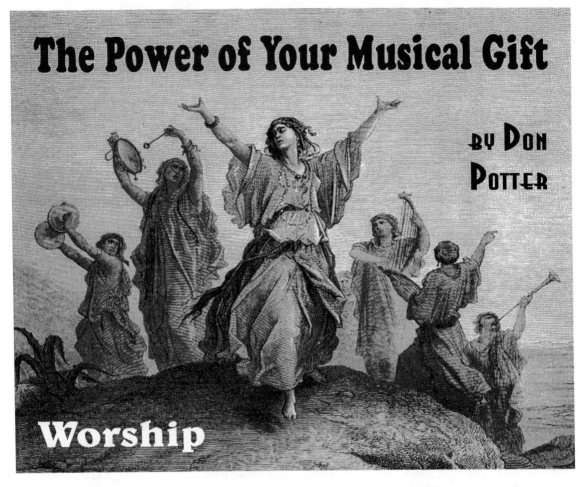

Worship

All Scripture references KJV unless otherwise indicated.

Let me explain for a minute what life a gifted musician might be coming out of, if he has come to know the Lord or in the case of one raised in the church, what life he might be trying to get into. I am drawing much of this from my own experience. I've been a professional musician for thirty six years. Professional means someone who has, on occasion, made a few dollars playing music he hopes others will like.

I found my hope in Jesus when I was thirty five. By the time I got saved I had already played musically, with some success, for twenty two years. I had learned many things along the way as a musician, such as how to please men; how to be the life of the party; how to use my gift to make friends and influence people; how to not be a responsible person because I was too busy being creative;

how to make music a god; and under no conditions would I ever let anyone see that I didn't know what I was doing. There are many more things I learned to do with this gift but that would bring too much attention to the works of the devil, so I will not go any further.

By the time a musician has played for twenty years, he or she has probably gained an understanding of how to manipulate the emotions of others, because that is essentially what we are called to do with our music. If it does not influence emotions it will not be successful. Many musicians are different and strange to those who are not musicians, so they often have a hard time getting along in life. Because of this, when they learn that their gift can manipulate others, they can be very tempted to use it for their own purposes. In fact, that is what the secular music world teaches musicians that they should do with their gift. In many cases it is the difference between survival or the death of their musical success, which to them is nothing less than their identity.

These are all things which the devil and the world try to do to both music and musicians. In Ezekiel we see that Lucifer was the worship leader in heaven. Music was his domain there, and after he fell he has been determined to keep that domain. Music is one of his most powerful tools for keeping men under his dominion, and for leading them into self-worship or idolatry which keeps them from the true worship of God. Therefore, when we use music for a true worship of God, and break free from all of the evil yokes that have been placed on music and musicians, we are taking a very powerful tool out of the hands of the enemy. Without question, music is one of the important battle grounds between light and darkness.

> **While we may cast out demons with a word, we must wrestle with principalities to displace them.**

While we may cast out demons with a word, we must wrestle with principalities to displace them. Satan is the ultimate principality, and music is one of his ultimate weapons. That is why music was used as a weapon of warfare in the Scriptures, even to the point where the musicians marched in front of the army (see II Chronicles 20:20-23). However, we must recognize that there will be a mighty struggle over the power of music, and for the soul of every musician. That is why it is important for us to understand the strongholds that Satan has established through music, and over music, and how they can affect each of us.

Many musicians begin their professional career by playing "top forty" night clubs. Top forty songs are the ones which have proved popular with the world, so the club owner knows these will make his customers happy. But more than that, it will be the music that will make them drink a lot. The main point is to keep them coming back. If you don't comply to these demands, you will be fired as a musician at the typical night club, which is one of the most common places for the musician to use his gift.

The top forty musician will usually start experiencing some frustration when he finds out he is not allowed to be creative or offer anything that could threaten the club owners' hope of selling drinks. If the band is too loud and plays too long, the people will dance too much and not drink enough. If the band is too soft, the crowd will go home or to another club. One must learn how to control the people just right to be successful. To the employer of this type of musician, controlling the people is more important that making good music.

After the top forty night clubs, the other options for musicians are quite limited. Unless you have an extraordinary gift which allows you to write some original music and perform it for a listening audience, you will have to get some other work to make an income. A few can become studio musicians, others road players with a traveling act. A very tiny percentage may be able to gain part time work with a symphony. Those are about the limits for musicians who want to work in their field. This means that to do what you feel called to do you must still comply with all of the demands put on you, and will have your own creativity frustrated. To escape this, your own creative gift will have to be recognized, but there is hardly any way for it to be since there is no place for it to be expressed. This breeds a deep frustration in many musicians, and also an almost constant drive toward self-promotion. Of course, this is contrary to the reason for which the gift was given to us—to worship God. In this way Satan has been able to keep strong yokes on most who would enter what he still believes is his domain—music.

This also breeds a fierce competition among musicians. Because there is such competition, the music companies are able to sign musicians and artists for such low pay that most are also constantly struggling just to pay the rent and eat. Even those who have top hits must stay on the road most of the time to make a living and pay their bills. That is why few artists stay on top for more than a couple of years. They burn out quickly and their creativity is sapped by the system.

Naturally all of this bleeds over into the musician's family life. For many the choice is to either lose their families or quit the music business altogether. If they choose their families over their gifts, they will often spend their lives wondering what might have happened had they stayed in music, or just resenting all those who look like they're making it. Sounds like a pleasant life doesn't it?

I am only touching the surface of what a complicated life the gift of creativity can be. Since the gift was given for the express purpose of blessing God, by offering up to Him the fruit of the seed He planted, then any other use of it is a misuse. That does not mean one can never be successful using their gifts in secular venues anymore than we should say that a gifted carpenter should only use his gift to build churches. It does mean that we must first offer our gift to God, and let Him decide if making us famous is what will bring glory to His name.

As stated, the "top forty" musician does not make up the entire music world, but his plight is typical and is a good example of what almost every musician faces when trying to use that which is a love of their life—playing music.

Discerning the Gifts

It is believed by many Christian musicians that all one had to do with his or her gift was to do Christian things with it. Get a Christian record contract and get famous for the work of the Lord. That's a nice thought, but so far very few are really sold out to whatever the Lord wants for them. The same way that the world promotes, and uses music for manipulation and actual self-promotion, has become the way of much of the Christian music business as well. The amount of records that the world sells has become the goal of the Christian business. The idea of bringing the gospel to the lost through radio may have been a motive used by many to justify this self-promotion, but that is usually just a self-delusion to justify the sin of self-promotion. The Truth is too challenging for the "top forty" masses, so the truth must be compromised out of the music to make it the way many want to, supposedly for the sake of the truth. The fact is, singing about the reality of Jesus working in your life, and the Holy Spirit convicting us of our sin, does not sell, even to a Christian audience.

So we have done the next best thing. We glorify the gifts of the Christian. Who can sing the highest note. Who has more control over their voice. Who is able to play the hottest lick on their instrument, etc. And all of these envious ideas came from years of listening to the music produced by the world. Just being able to do all of these things will not lift up the name of Jesus.

I have played on many mainstream hit records, and later on some Christian projects, and there is often more reality and truth on the music of the world than that produced by many popular Christian artists. This is probably the reason why the young Christian hopefuls have set their sights on being like the musicians of the world. This is not to say that there are no Christian artists with a heart for God, and some are doing their best to be faithful to the call on their lives; it's just not promoted in the business of selling CDs, and is actually very rarely found, even in Christian music.

Is Trying to Get Famous a Good Idea?

Isaiah 2:12 says, **"For the day of the LORD of hosts shall be upon every one that is proud and lofty, and upon every one that is lifted up; and he shall be brought low."** It's interesting that this Scripture does not try to make allowances for certain people or things. It says EVERY ONE that is lifted up. That means, not only am I in trouble for lifting myself up, but I'm in trouble for letting myself be lifted up unless it is by God.

First Peter 5:6 says, **"Humble yourselves therefore under the mighty hand of God, that he may exalt you in due time."** This Scripture would make a lot of people in the music business uncomfortable, but it is the truth of God's word, and if we are going to serve Him we must live by His words, not the ways of the world, even if those ways will make us "successful" quicker.

It has been my experience over the many years of playing, that the truly gifted musicians are not as interested in lifting themselves up as much as improving on their instrument. Though often the only way to survive in the business was to promote yourself, the truly gifted musicians are not nearly as interested in trying to get famous. Then who is trying to get them famous? Good question. The answer is record companies.

Record companies for the most part do not have musicians as their executives. So what is left is the competitive sale of the creative efforts of non-self-promoting people. Since it is easier to sell someone that is interested in lifting themselves up, it's better for business to find those kinds of acts, and let the non-self-promoting-only-interested-in-getting-better ones go. That is why top hits and top acts are seldom produced by those

who really are the most gifted. It has been my experience that those who are bent on getting famous are often not very good players or performers, but they do "sing the tune" that the record companies want to hear. Fame for the artist converts to record sales. Period.

So over the years the generally challenging quality of music has been slowly decreasing, because the ones that were bent on getting famous, have been doing so. This meant that glitter had to increase because the substance decreased. And glitter is what has attracted many to sell all for a moment in the spot light. Again I must qualify this by saying there are many great musicians and singers that are recording and doing quality work, but there are just not many in the mainstream of the music business, and it is getting more and more rare.

When the quality of talent started to decrease, the demand for entertainment went up. The almighty audience wanted something to move them. So like any good businessmen, the companies gave 'em what they wanted. If the music wasn't good, you just showed more skin. If the artist was ugly, you fired them and got somebody sexy. If the sexy act is not gifted, you fix them up with high-tech equipment. You can see where I'm going with this.

Our artists and entertainers are a lot more imaginary then most suspect. We are not seeing what we are seeing, and we are not hearing what we are hearing. Still once in a while, a talented one gets through the maze. But for that talented one to survive, he must add glitter to his act, because it has now become expected, and is actually interpreted as a sign of success. And because the bad performers have been electronically made good, the good performers now sound inferior when nothing is done to their records. The prince of the air really does have a stronghold over what gets played on the air.

This is only a brief explanation of some of the experiences a musician can go through before he or she comes to the church. It can take a long time for them to go through the process of having their minds renewed, or to be healed of all of the spiritual and emotional wounds they have suffered. We will seldom get a musician who comes to the church who is a perfect worshiper of God, but this is their calling if they have been musically gifted by God, and it is worth paying the price to get them free and healed, but that does not mean it will be easy.

Musicians in the Tabernacle of David

Now in contrast to that way of life, we have the Levitical priesthood in the time of king David. There were thirty eight thousand Levites and all of them had made their own instruments, played from the earliest ages, knew the Scriptures by heart by the age of thirty (see I Chronicles 23:3), and all of their needs were provided for them by the church. After thirty years they were ready to be chosen by lot, not by talent or self-promotional skills (see I Chronicles 24:31, 25:1). Then they were ready to minister to the Lord, prophesy on their instruments with their gifts of music. They were commanded by David to minister to the presence of God continually (see I Chronicles 16:37). Their duties were to carry the burden of the presence of God (see I Chronicles 15:2), and to minister to Him in the tabernacle.

Only four thousand of the thirty eight thousand were picked to minister in the tabernacle on the instruments of music (see I Chronicles 23:5), and they went in shifts for twenty-four hours a day. They all qualified for the job, but only four thousand were chosen. The rest of the Levites did the daily things that were needed in the tabernacle, such as keeping the doors, taking care of the grounds and the tent itself, making sure all the sacrifices that were offered were unblemished, and, in general, ministering to the people as well as the needs of the tabernacle. Needless to say, their responsibilities were essential to the dwelling place of God, but most of them were not doing what was probably the chief love of their life but a small portion of the time. Out of those who were willing to serve, four thousand would be chosen at a time to lead the worship.

How awesome it must have been to be in the presence of God continually, much less to be faced with ministering to His presence. The quality of praise must have been the best that it could be. This sheds a completely different light on the true role of a musician. They served God. They sometimes served Him with their instruments, but if they were not chosen to do that, they served Him in other ways. But above all, they served, they were not there to be served. Somewhere between the Levitical priesthood and the "top forty" musician, things got sideways.

Woe to those who rise early in the morning to run after their drinks, who stay up late at night till they are inflamed with wine.

They have harps and lyres at their banquets, tambourines and flutes and wine, but they have no regard for the deeds of the LORD, no respect for the work of his hands (Isaiah 5:11-12 NIV).

The word *banquets* here means a place where people drink and gather together. Sounds like a top forty night club. This also sounds like what might have happened to the job of musician. It's very much like the club owner and the people that had little regard for the deeds of God. Gifting, whether used for good or evil, will be determined by the one that it is trusted to. There is a system out there ready to devour all who will serve it, but the choice is still ours whether to serve this system or not.

It is easy to understand why most musicians prefer success over service, acceptance over rejection, so they will do what ever is demanded of them. However, it is up to each of us to determine whether we will compromise and bow down to the devil and his ways, or serve the Lord His way. However, the church does not always make this choice an easy one. The reason is that the system that rules over much of the church, and over popular Christian music, is the way of the world and not the way of God. It is therefore understandable why so many Christian musicians fall to the other traps and sins of the world, since there is often little to distinguish what they do with their gifts in church from what they do with them in the world. This is not to justify their fall, but it is understandable.

The Meaning of Entertainment

"Entertain" means, "to hold together; to keep the interest of and give pleasure; to divert and amuse." Because the afterfix -*tain* often means to keep out, or to hold up, such as in de-*tain*, "entertain" can be the counter to "entering-in." The prefix *a*- is also usually used as a negative, or counter, as "amusement" is actually a counter word to "musing," or deeply reflecting on something. That is of course the effect of entertainment and amusement; it occupies us without requiring us to think, or to enter in ourselves. Music can do the same thing. If music is to be used to help bring the church into the presence of the Lord in worship, it must be used to help us enter in, not entertain. There can be a subtle difference between the two, but the ultimate result of each is profoundly different.

True worship does not require us to disengage our minds, but rather to focus them on Him. In effect, we do worship that which has our attention. If when we are worshiping our attention is more on the music than on the Lord, the music has usurped the place of the Lord, and an idol that has eclipsed Him as the focus of our attention. Now much of the church seems to have tried to remedy this by playing only the most dull music which is not in danger of capturing anyone's attention, but this is actually only demeaning to the glory of the Lord. When we really begin to see the glory of the Lord there will not be any music that can distract us, regardless of how wonderful it is. If we are called to worship Him with our music, we must give Him our very best, but we must understand that the music is the sacrifice, the offering, the One we are offering it to is the reason for the music.

We can call ourselves Christians, but if our attention really is on the ways of the devil, or on self-promotion, then we are not worshiping God in Spirit and in truth. If we are going to use our musical gifts to worship God, we must learn to "muse deeply" on what our singing and playing in the temple is accomplishing, or we may go on playing but the presense of the Lord will have departed.

In David's tabernacle the musicians were instructed to minister to the Lord. When was this changed to minister to the people? When did the demands of the people become a priority over ministering to God? The Levitical priests who were not chosen to minister in music were the ones that came out of the tabernacle to minister to the people. The musicians stayed in the tabernacle continually offering thanks and praise to God.

What Did David Do?

First Chronicles 16:4 says, **"And he [David] appointed certain of the Levites to minister before the ark of the LORD, and to record, and to thank and praise the LORD God of Israel."** "Record" meant that scribes heard the new songs that were being offered to God in thanksgiving and they were written down. There are one hundred and fifty of these psalms in our Bible. Seventy three were written by David. Forty nine were anonymous. That means many new songs came forth unto God that were recorded, but no one knew who was singing them. When the king came in the tabernacle for his worship time and began singing his prayers and praise to God, the scribes knew it was him. Thus, much of what David offered in song to God was recorded. The same happened for Asaph and others, but there were also others that came from unknown worshipers, but they were good enough to become canon Scripture.

This implies that it is right that even that which is meant to be used in worship to God be recorded and shared with the people. However, this was not done just to bless the people, but rather to also stir the people to worship God. In David's tabernacle the people were also allowed into the courts of the Lord to praise Him. Anyone could come into His courts with praise as long as he entered His gates with thanksgiving.

In this same way our music that is truly an offering to God should stir the people, but not toward ourselves or our gift. Even though each thirty year veteran musician was obviously playing his very best before the God of Israel, he was doing it for the God of Israel, not recognition. Christian musicians should be the best, and offer the best to God, but for His sake, not our own. As the Lord Himself made clear in John 7:18:

> He who speaks from himself seeks his own glory; but He who is seeking the glory of the one who sent Him, He is true, and there is no unrighteousness in Him (NAS).

What Does the New Testament Say?

In 1 Corinthians 14:26 Paul wrote,

> What is the outcome then, brethren? When you assemble, each one has a psalm, has a teaching, has a revelation, has a tongue, has an interpretation. Let all things be done for edification (NAS).

The word translated "psalm" here means, "the old songs to which new hymns and praises are added." Paul sounds like he is instructing the same thing that David was in the tabernacle. But now we have the extra advantage of the old hymns and the new song of praise. The new song has more to do with singing what's in your heart to God.

I know this all sounds like disorder after Paul instructs us to be orderly. But if we can remove from our minds the idea of stage and performance in front of people in the church, and know that we are all just worshipers of God, then I won't care what you are singing unto the Lord, and you won't even know what I'm singing to Him, because we are not focusing on one another but on Him. One doesn't have to have a microphone to be able to worship God with the new song.

Could We Remove the Stage?

Does the idea of a stage and performance in the church come from the Scriptures? No. It comes from the world. I have watched many people completely change their personalities when faced with the task of getting on stage and singing or preaching to others. This is like saying that the reality of their own true personality was not acceptable in front of the masses. It is what has become known as a TV personality. Who taught us that? Why do we think we have to imitate it? Now there are some practical reasons for having a stage, especially for preaching or ministering in large rooms. The remedy may not be to remove the physical stage as much as the stage mentality in our heart, but sometimes it may mean removing the physical stage.

If we follow the lead that Jesus left for us, we see someone who always taught the truth and said whatever He was told by His Father. That sometimes offended most who were present. I can't imagine any show-biz tactics being used by the Lord of Lords. Isaiah 53 says He had no stately form or majesty that we should look upon Him. His strategy was truth, not appearances.

When He spoke to the multitudes in Matthew 5, He was addressing some of the most oppressed people on the earth. They were slaves in their own land, poor and deprived of the freedom that most men enjoyed, and filled with anger, hate and hopelessness. They were waiting for Messiah to come and crush their oppressors so they could be free again in the Lord. And His speech begins with, "**blessed are the poor in spirit**" (**Matthew 5:3**). He probably didn't draw a lot of applause for that sermon. Come to think of it, He probably did not get much applause for any of His sermons. Would He now if He preached in our church?

The performance spirit is ingrained deeper than we think. As long as a congregation is sitting in judgment, like an audience does at a concert, those who get in front of them will be faced with the age old problem of *acting* like someone they believe will be acceptable to the audience. Then it becomes a battle of the opinions. If opinion is held in higher regard than discernment, we as the congregation will reward those who meet our expectations, rejecting all that does not measure up—and not much of what is truly God will measure up to our present appetites for entertainment over substance. In doing this, we get our desires met, or the desired results from the people, but are we getting the results we need from God?

For the time will come when men will not put up with sound doctrine. Instead, to suit their own desires, they will gather around them a great number of teachers to say what their itching ears want to hear (II Timothy 4:3 NIV).

Will this be what is written about our generation? We know that the Lord returns for a church that worships Him, not the world, or those who worship it. We are all making the choice now if we are going to be that church whose passion for Him compels Him to come for us. Worship is one of the powerful ways that has been given to us to express our love for Him, and in some ways even prepare our hearts for Him. Those who recapture the true meaning of worship, and the true use for which music was created, will have displaced the evil one from one of his most powerful strongholds, but even more importantly, captured the attention of our Lord. He will draw near to those who draw near to Him, and worship, in all of its different facets, is how we draw near to Him.

Don Potter, and his wife Christine, live in Nashville, TN. Don has produced or played with such artists as Chuck Mangione, The Judds and Wynonna, as well as being a sought after recording studio musician. Don and Christine have an intense passion to see the Tabernacle of David restored with true Davidic worship.

CHRONICLES

Snapshots from History

These historical briefs were compiled by students at *The MorningStar School of Ministry*. Of course, it is impossible to do justice to these great names from church history in such short briefs, but it is our hope that it will stir some of our readers to more in-depth studies of those to whom we all owe so much.

All Scripture references NAS unless otherwise indicated.

JOHN CALVIN

by Mary Rose Helbling

John Calvin was a man to whom the modern day church owes much, but also a man whose weaknesses can instruct us. He was born in Noyon, Picardy, France on July 10, 1509. Calvin's early life was shaped by his fortunate connections with sons of noblemen. Tutored in the home of the de Hangest family, Calvin forged a lasting friendship with Claude, later an abbot at Noyon to whom Calvin dedicated his first book.

When Calvin was 14 years old, he, three of the de Hangest boys, and their tutor went to the University of Paris. Five years later, he received a Master of Arts in Theology. Instead of continuing his theological education, Calvin switched to pursue a law degree. This was due to his father's dispute with the cathedral chapter and desire to see his son involved in a more lucrative career than becoming a cleric. It seems as though Calvin was only being an obedient child to his father's wishes—for three years later, after his father died, Calvin turned his heart once again, to the study of language and literature.

Sometime around the mid-1530s, Calvin's life was interrupted by God. As he states, "Since I was more stubbornly addicted to the superstitions of the Papacy than to be easily drawn out of so deep a mire, God subdued my heart—too stubborn for my age—to docility by a sudden conversion." Whether at that point Calvin was actually converted or not, it was evident afterward that he was a different man. Before, he was a young, brilliant humanist, and after, an intensely dedicated student of truth.

Shortly after this turning point, Calvin became frustrated with the Roman Catholic church in France. While Reformation was sweeping across Germany and Switzerland, it seemed hopeless that change would come in the midst of the country's tolerant Christian humanism. Like many moves of God, there was resistance against France also tasting the Reformation's new freedom. Because of France's hardened position, Calvin left the Roman Catholic Church and France, and became an exile in Basle. He began to formulate his theology, repudiating the papacy and siding with the passionate minority of persecuted evangelicals when he was just 25 years old. At 27, he published the first edition of his "Institute Religionus Christianae" (Institution of Christian Religion), written in Latin for scholarly readers throughout the continent, and which became one of the great classics of Christian literature.

Calvin just desired an opportunity to think and read, giving no thought, at first, to public leadership. Although he saw himself as no more than an introverted scholar, he could not keep silent. Those who knew of his views pursued him to inquire about "the purer doctrine." After visiting a friend in Italy, Calvin intended to return to Strasbourg and resume his writing. Here, God again interrupted his life. Because of the war between Francis I and Charles V, Calvin was forced to take a detour through Geneva. It would be in this sizable city of 10,000 that Calvin would leave his mark upon the world, causing many to refer to Geneva as the "Protestant Rome."

While in Geneva, Calvin met Guillaume Farel, a fiery Protestant preacher who had single-handedly secured the churches in the city for evangelical preaching. At the time, there was a power struggle between the city and the dukes of Savoy, whose control of Geneva's bishops was becoming tiresome for its citizens. They were ready for a change. In 1536, Farel persuaded Calvin to stay and implement the new Protestant faith within the churches. Calvin reluctantly agreed. In his own words, he stated that Farel proceeded "to utter an imprecation that God would curse my retirement, and the tranquillity of the studies which I sought if I should withdraw and refuse to give assistance, when the necessity was so urgent. By this imprecation I was so stricken with terror that I desisted from the journey which I had undertaken."

Two years later turmoil again arose in Geneva. Farel and Calvin were forced to flee over religious disputes with Berne, a city that had earlier supported Farel as he had preached throughout Geneva, but now attempted to impose their rites upon the new reformed churches. Calvin joined a French refugee colony in Strasbourg and for three years organized a French congregation, lectured and wrote liturgy, as well as a small book of psalms set to music.

In 1539, Rome appealed to Geneva to return to the fold. The unstable city then turned to Calvin to enlist him for their reply to the letter. Calvin did not want to return. "I would prefer a hundred other deaths to that cross," he later stated. But finally, on September 2, 1541, Calvin returned to Geneva. His intended stay of a few months stretched into years. Calvin never lived to see his homeland again, Geneva being his permanent residence until his death in 1564.

After returning to Geneva, Calvin created the Ecclesiastical Ordinances, which was a system of discipline, preaching, worship, and instruction that incorporated the ministry of pastors, teachers (doctors), elders, and deacons. Minor offenses to Calvin's set of laws and moral regulations were handled by the elders and ministers. Serious offenses were sent to the full council. Calvin's reputation and constant involvement made him the leader not only of the Geneva church, but ultimately of the whole city.

Calvin had abhorred the tyranny of Rome, but he himself later became guilty of nearly the same excesses, and many historians have called him "The Tyrant of Geneva." His position was precarious, often being insulted or threatened by those who preferred looser morals and liberal opinions. Calvin responded by continued preaching, writing and contending, often harshly, with his opponents. He encouraged the burning of witches. Even eminent men were not safe from Calvin's control. Jacques Gruet was beheaded for blasphemy, treason, and a threat to the ministers. Jerome Bolsec, a physician who attacked Calvin's doctrine of predestination, was banished. A heretic who also was an anti-Trinitarian was burned at the stake.

Calvin had made a mistake similar to that of Peter's. Peter had also claimed that he would never be like the other disciples and deny Jesus. He ended up doing just what he said he would not do. In Acts 10:34, Peter contended that through Christ people of all nations could be saved, through their fear of God and not by works of the Law. Later, Peter rendered his statement meaningless when he refused to eat with the Gentiles when his Jewish brethren were present (see Galatians 2:11-16). Peter said one thing, but did the opposite. Oftentimes, we become that which we too harshly judge in others. This does not mean that we overlook sin or mistakes, but we must be careful how we judge, just as Paul warned in Galatians 6:1:

> **Brethren, even if a man is caught in *any* trespass, you who are spiritual, *restore* such a one in a spirit of gentleness; each one looking to yourself, lest you too be tempted.**

Political opponents to Calvin's authority were defeated over time. Laws became more restrictive and the punishment more exacting. Political authority rested mainly in the "Little Council." Despite these repressive elements in the regime, it was balanced by the great attention given to education. From 1558 onward, the Academy of Geneva birthed Calvinism throughout all parts of Europe. In his forties, Calvin continued to write his commentaries and treatises, despite his failing health. Finally, on May 27, 1564, Calvin died in Geneva at the age of 55. His contribution to society was not only his theological doctrine, but his successors. Theodorus Beza and Giovanni Diodato were responsible for translating the Italian Bible, whose popularity later withstood the publishing of the King James translation.

John Calvin had his weaknesses, but he was still mightily used by God to move the church from one point to another. When moving a monolithic church structure as large as Rome was in his day, there were bound to be some mistakes made by the newly birthed reformed churches.

Mary Rose Helbling is a MorningStar School of Ministry student, originally from Cincinnati, Ohio. Her heart's desire is to see the church walk in more freedom in the creative arts, intercession and women's ministry. Mary Rose resides in Charlotte, North Carolina.

JOHN WESLEY

by Cory McClure

John Wesley was a common man with an uncommon dedication to God. He was not tall in stature, but he spiritually towered over the other men of God in his day. Throughout his life, his humility, dedication, and insatiable desire for the truth helped to change the course of church history in England and around the world.

Wesley's father was a rector for the Church of England and his mother was a woman not common to the times. She openly disagreed with her husband concerning her loyalties to the Crown. She was fiercely loyal to the exiled King James II, while Mr. Wesley demanded loyalty to King William. Due to this difference, Mr. Wesley refused to share the same bed with his wife until she capitulated. She would not. John Wesley had not been born yet and the future looked bleak. However, the following year King William died, thereby bringing unity of loyalty back into the household. Shortly thereafter, on June 17, 1703, John Wesley was born.

The Wesleys were a very poor family. Being a rector provided a guaranteed income, but not one that would comfortably provide for his rather large family. As John grew, he was taught the Scriptures primarily by his mother. He was required to read and write Scripture every day as part of his education. His father encouraged him to go into the ministry. John had studied hard and knew the Scriptures. He was a good speaker and seemed destined for the church, but he did not want to go into the ministry unless he felt the calling of the Lord. However, after seeing few other opportunities available to him, he decided to seek "Holy Orders" in 1724, partly to ensure himself a livelihood and partly to lead a "more strict life."

As a student at Oxford, he read "The Christian Pattern" which revealed to him that true religion was seated in the heart, and God's law extended to all our thoughts as well as words and actions. As comforting as these words were to Wesley, he still didn't feel the assurance that Jesus was always present in his heart. Thus he determined to make himself worthy of Jesus.

John was ordained on September 19, 1725, and began his ministry as the Fellow of Lincoln on March 17, 1726. He quickly became known in the region for his oratory ability and devotion to the Bible. He disciplined himself to rise early in the morning for prayer and devotions. Every hour on the hour he would take a moment to lift a prayer into the heavenlies. He began to preach this methodology of devotion unto God. This began to offend his friends and fellow clergy and they began to ridicule him.

In 1730, Wesley began to go to the prisons and preach to the thieves and ruffians. They were enthusiastic and listened to his messages with great interest. No clergyman had ever come to the prison before to preach to the prisoners. Wesley began to disciple many of them, encouraging them that "every hour of the day had its proper use, whether for study, devotions, exercise, or charity." He was teaching them that method and order should be a way of life. However, his friends at Oxford did not agree with his discipline. They felt it ridiculous to visit prisoners and the poor, because of their doctrine of predestination. However, Wesley was beginning to have doubts about that very doctrine.

By 1732, the term "Methodist" was being used to describe Wesley's form of ministry. He felt mocked by this term, because he had no intention of dividing himself from the Church of England. However, in 1736 his life would be profoundly impacted and changed forever.

Colonel Oglethorpe, a close friend of Wesley, had been to America and was concerned about the new colonies, specifically the southern colonies of Georgia and South Carolina. When Oglethorpe asked Wesley if he would like to go to America as a missionary to the Indians, Wesley quickly agreed. Wesley's primary purpose in going was the hope of saving his own soul by learning the true sense of the gospel by preaching it to the Indians. He believed that his ultimate salvation depended upon good works as opposed to faith. On the boat going to Georgia he met a group of Germans that would change his life and theology forever. They were Moravian missionaries sent from the estate of Count Zinzendorf.

During the trip, Wesley began to notice the Moravians, and in particular their sense of peace, regardless of the circumstances. They suffered without complaint through the rough seas, cramped conditions, and bad food. In contrast, the Moravians noticed Wesley's strict regimen and routine and thought it was for the purpose of

gaining merit with God. Through a series of discussions, the Moravians offered Wesley the great Reformation doctrine of Justification by Faith. Wesley thought it foolish at the time, but the seed was planted in his heart.

On February 7, 1738, after his return to England from America, Wesley met Peter Bohler, who was on his way to South Carolina as a Moravian missionary. After many days and numerous debates with Wesley, Bohler convinced Wesley of the doctrine of Justification by Faith. Though he was convinced of the doctrine, he was concerned whether he should preach it, because he felt he had so little faith himself. Bohler encouraged him to preach faith, saying, "Preach faith until you have it. And then, because you have it, you will preach faith." This was difficult for Wesley to do, because it required faith to preach something he wasn't sure he had, though he knew scripturally it was correct. This began to break down his rigid traditions.

The following year, he began to preach against the doctrine of predestination. At one point, in the city of Newgate, while preaching to a crowd of prisoners, he declared that if he was speaking the truth of Justification by Faith that God would manifest Himself through signs and wonders. Immediately, the power of God fell on all who were there. Due to Wesley's new doctrine, he was being shunned by the churches in the area. At this point in his ministry people were coming out to see him in large numbers. After he was free from preaching in the church, God moved him out into the countryside where the number of people he could preach to increased dramatically.

In 1742 Wesley published his doctrine of Christian Perfection, which provoked much debate over the next couple of centuries, but he had recovered a part of the Christian experience in victorious living which would influence churches all over the world. Wesley's teachings and preaching continued to attract more people. However, it also continued to upset the leaders in the Church of England. Wesley therefore came under great persecution wherever he went.

During the 1750s through the 1760s, Wesley continued to build his "societies" of followers and developed schools and orphanages. His preaching and teaching took him throughout Britain, and his writings and publications were being read around the world by all social classes. This was unique, because few of the "lower class" people could understand the writings of the day, but Wesley wrote in such a way that the common man could understand what was being said. This brought an understanding of God's word to the common man, which ignited revival fires throughout the land.

At this time, the Enlightenment Movement was beginning, so Wesley combined his writings with abridged versions of Christian classics to form the "Christian Library." Some of his abridged writings were inaccurate and slanted toward his doctrines. This caused him trouble later.

In 1784, he made a decision which would change his legacy in the church forever. Thomas Coke, a disciple under Wesley, was headed for America to oversee the "societies" there. Wesley ordained Coke and gave him a certificate as general superintendent of the Methodists in America, effectively beginning the Methodist denomination in America and formally splitting from the Church of England. In this one move, Wesley took upon himself the authority to ordain and release leaders, previously only allowed by the Church, and formed a denomination that would sweep the American colonies.

Wesley's life is a testament of single-minded pursuit for biblical truth, uncompromising faith, and dedication to spiritual discipline. Though persecuted most of his ministerial life, he would not waiver or compromise his beliefs. Wesley's books, sermons, letters, and personal example combined faith, holy living, and Christian knowledge in a new way, thus giving new life to theology and practice in Britain and around the world.

Currently a student at the MorningStar School of Ministry, Cory McClure is dedicated to the "equipping of the saints for the work of the ministry, for the edifying of the body of Christ" (Ephesians 4:12). Before coming to Charlotte he was the church administrator at Abundant Life Christian Center in Tucson, Arizona. He and his wife, Kena, and their two children live in Charlotte, NC.

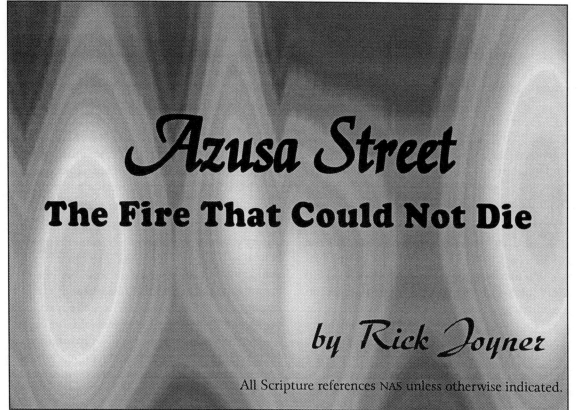

Azusa Street
The Fire That Could Not Die

by Rick Joyner

All Scripture references NAS unless otherwise indicated.

Over the last two millenniums the church has experienced many revivals, renewals, and reformation movements. Each has added a wealth of experience and understanding to the ways in which the Holy Spirit moves to reveal Jesus to His church, and to those in darkness. Almost every one of these movements has been progressive in the restoration of biblical truth to the church, truth that was either lost or was neglected during the Middle Ages. Without question, one of the most significant of all of these movements has been the Pentecostal Revival of the twentieth century.

It is impossible to understand the present state of Christianity without understanding both the past and continuing impact of the Pentecostal Movement. To even call what began at Azusa Street just a revival would be to obscure its true importance. It was a revival, but it was also a renewal and a reformation of the church as well. With the possible exception of Luther's Reformation, there probably has not been another movement in church history which has had a greater overall impact on the entire church.

This impact is not only continuing, it is continuing to increase. Through the Pentecostal Revival, and the subsequent neo-Pentecostal movements spawned from it such as the Charismatic Renewal, already more ministers of the gospel have been ordained, more missionaries have been sent out, more churches have been planted, and more people have been brought to salvation than through any other movement in church history. If the present rate of growth is sustained, soon the numbers of those impacted by this renewal will eclipse the totals of all other movements combined.

To understand how the essence of this movement has been able to mature, while at the same time staying responsive to new moves of the Spirit, is important for every spiritual leader. Many of its churches, and even whole denominations, have continued to reach for greater spiritual power while at the same time sinking their roots deeper into sound biblical truth, making necessary corrections and adjustments while maintaining a forward momentum. Of course this should be the norm, but it has in fact been the exception to the nature of movements. Understanding what has enabled much of the Pentecostal Movement to achieve this is certainly one of the most important lessons we can learn.

It is often hard to imagine as we read the great impact of many of the previous spiritual movements, but most of them lasted a very short time. Rarely has a movement stayed on the cutting edge of what God is doing for more than a decade, and more often it is but a year or two. Even the apostolic move of the first century church faded rapidly into an increasing apostasy shortly after the death of its first leaders. However, defying all of the previous norms for such movements, the Pentecostal Movement has continued to keep moving for almost a century, and there is no end to its continued advance in sight. It is not only still increasing, impacting millions more each year, but its *rate* of growth is still increasing. Taken as a group, the Pentecostal/Charismatic Movements are now the second largest category in all of Christianity. If their present rate of growth is sustained, they will, in just a few years, outnumber the rest of Christianity *combined.*

Of course, there are many individuals, churches, and even whole denominations that were birthed out of this movement which have stopped moving. In many places one can only find the remnants of the past glory, with little or no continuing fire. Even so, around the world there are multitudes of Pentecostal/Charismatic churches that are ablaze with the presence and activity of God. In countries where the greatest advances of the gospel are now taking place, Pentecostals are usually found at the vanguard.

Like most others, the Pentecostal Movement had a spectacular beginning, followed by upheaval from within, and persecution from without. Many mistakes were made that threatened to sidetrack the entire movement, but most of these were resolved in such a way that they gave even greater stability to the movement, enabling it to continue its advance. The lessons we learn from these situations can help any advancing church or movement.

Understanding the mistakes made by others can help us to avoid the same traps, but before we become too concerned with how to avoid the traps of revival, we probably need to know how to start one! Because the most important step in any journey is the first one, understanding how true moves of God begin is crucial. We will also usually find that, just as the genetic code that determines what a grown man will look like is set at conception, the "genetic code" of entire movements is usually set even before their birth. One of the reasons why the Pentecostal Movement is so unique in church history is because it had such a unique beginning. Much of what can be recognized as its present nature was actually already established by the time it was born.

The Beginning

Foundations are important. The strength and longevity of everything that is built will be affected by the strength of the foundation it is built upon. The church that is built upon the foundation of Jesus Christ will prevail just as He did. Any other foundation will have different results. The apostle Paul also warned that we must be careful how we build upon the foundation. He declared that all "wood, hay and stubble" will be burned up, and that only "gold, silver and precious stones will remain." Therefore, in our studies of churches or movements we should look for things that have proven to be "wood, hay and stubble," which do not last, as well as those things which have proven to be "gold, silver and precious stones," which do last.

The beginning of the Pentecostal Movement is usually marked from the outpouring of the Holy Spirit at Azusa Street in 1906. There were a number of powerful ministries and movements which both experienced and promulgated the baptism of the Holy Spirit prior to Azusa Street, but none of them had the continuing impact that this one did. It was a true beginning, and it added something to the advancing church that has lasted. The movement has changed, and now has many different streams, but one can recognize what originated at Azusa as the source in most of the moves of God that have set the course of Christianity in this century.

Two Witnesses

William J. Seymour and Frank Bartleman are the two names that are most often recognized as those who were used to start the Azusa Street Revival. They were different in many ways, but they were both young men who had an uncommon desire to know the Lord and see His power restored to the church. Seymour was the unquestioned leader of the revival, and he had the authority on earth, but Bartleman was the intercessor who had authority with God.

Because these men were so different, their stories give us two very different views of the Azusa Street Revival, but ones that do compliment each other to give us a more complete picture. As Seymour was the actual leader of the Azusa Street Revival, we will begin with his story. But first we must go back a little further.

The Grandfather

Charles Fox Parham (1873-1929) presided over a Bible school in Topeka, Kansas. He was a true spiritual father, and many consider him the father of the modern Pentecostal Movement. Even though he would later reject many of his own spiritual children, his part in this movement must be recognized and understood.

Parham was a seeker of God who was constantly challenged by what he viewed as the great chasm between biblical Christianity and the state of the church. He sought the Lord for what he considered to be true, biblical Christianity. As he was keeping a prayer vigil on New Year's Eve, he experienced the spiritual gift of "speaking in tongues," or "glossolalia" in the early hours of January 1, 1901, the precise dawning of the Twentieth Century.

Speaking in tongues, or the use of other spiritual gifts, are by no means unique in church history. Many reformers and revivalists had such experiences. Even so, Parham's experience came at what could be called "the fulness of time," or a time that was ripe for the harvest of a recovered truth. His experience created a great deal of interest, mostly because of the dry and lifeless state of the church at the time. Parham was not known for emotionalism or exaggeration, but rather the opposite. He was conservative and resolute. This gave even more credibility to his experience.

A couple of years after his experience, Parham's health broke down and he was forced to move to Houston where he could stay with friends. His strength recovered and he began another Bible school in the Texas port city. William Seymour became one of his students, but because he was black, and Parham was a strict segregationist, he had to sit outside of the classroom and listen through a door that Parham would leave cracked open for him. Seymour wanted the Lord so much that he would embrace any humiliation to be close to what he felt the Lord was doing, and he was convinced that a new Pentecost was coming to the church.

William J. Seymour was born in Centerville, Louisiana on May 2, 1870. He was the son of former slaves, Simon and Phyllis Seymour. Even after gaining their freedom the Seymours had continued working on a plantation. Young William followed in their footsteps, growing strong in body and spirit, but receiving very little formal education. He taught himself to read so that he could read the Bible. Under the almost constant harassment of the Ku Klux Klan, and the oppressive Jim Crow laws, William became convinced that Jesus Christ was the only true liberator of men. After contracting small pox and losing one eye, he devoted himself to the ministry, proclaiming the gospel of the true liberty of all men through Jesus Christ.

Rejection Marks the Spot

In January of 1906, Seymour left Parham's school to pastor a mission congregation, without having received the baptism that he had sought for so long. Just a week after arriving he was rejected by congregational leaders of the mission who did not like his emphasis on the coming of a new Pentecost. One recurring theme in church history seems to be that most men and women of destiny arrive at their appointed place of destiny because of some level of rejection. We can see the same theme repeated in Scripture, such as in the lives of Joseph, Moses, David, and the Lord Jesus Himself, to name but a few. It seems as if a great disappointment with ourselves or men is simply a prerequisite to being used by God in a great way, especially to begin something new. It could even be said that learning to deal with rejection by men comes on the list of instructions for being a Christian. We should never be surprised by it, but keep our trust and attention on the Lord. He will use every such thing that happens to us for His own good, as well as ours.

Seymour recognized the hand of God in his rejection by the mission, and was content to form a little home prayer group which met regularly for several months. While in the middle of a ten day fast, Seymour and the others in this little group were dramatically baptized in the Holy Spirit, receiving the gift of tongues as well as other charismatic gifts.

Word spread "like fire in a dry wood" about what had happened at Seymour's little prayer group. This was probably caused by the remarkable ministry of Frank Bartleman, who had written a stream of articles and tracts, and constantly moved about the city exhorting churches and prayer groups to seek the Lord for a revival. He longed to see the Lord do in Los Angeles what He had recently done in Wales. After a time, Bartleman began to sense that what was to come to Los Angeles would be different from what was happening in Wales, and began to boldly prophesy the coming of "another Pentecost."

Bartleman's zeal for the Lord at this time was so great that his wife and friends began to fear for his life. He missed so much sleep and so many meals in order to pray that they did not think that he could last much longer. His response to their pleas for moderation was that he would rather die than not see revival.

He Is Still Born In a Stable

As soon as word got out about the experience that came upon Seymour's little prayer group, large crowds of interested people descended on them. To accommodate the large numbers of people, they were forced to rent a rundown old barn-like building in the middle of a black ghetto. At the time no one imagined that the little street that it was on, Azusa, would soon become one of the most famous addresses in the world.

The former mission had a dirt floor and was once used as a livery stable. Many remarked when they came that the Lord Himself had been born in just such a place. The rent was only $8.00 a month, and it could hold as many as 900 people. Even so, services were soon going almost around the clock to handle the hungry multitudes that were coming.

One of the most remarkable characteristics of this revival from the very beginning was the diversity of the people who were drawn to it. Some considered it unprecedented in church history. Within a week even a prominent Jewish rabbi announced his full support. Soon astounding healings and dramatic conversions were taking place almost daily. The church at the time was very dry, so each testimony went forth like sparks into a dry wood. Newspaper articles would fan the flames even more. Testimonies from the Welsh Revival had stirred multitudes to seek the Lord for revival in America, and the deplorable spiritual state of the country made her ready for it. Because of this, the fire spread faster than possibly any previous or subsequent revival in American history.

Seymour started a little paper to teach about the renewal, printing 5,000 copies. They were passed around until they fell apart. Soon he was printing 50,000, but there was no end to the demand.

Within weeks a steady stream of missionaries were coming from every continent on earth. Those who were on the front lines of the battle against the forces of darkness were the most acutely aware that they needed more power. Just as the Lord's own disciples were told that they would receive power to be His witnesses when the Holy Spirit came upon them, this had become the only hope for effective ministry that many of the missionaries had. They seized it like a drowning man grasps a lifesaver. They left Azusa with the power they needed, and soon gospel fires were burning brightly all over the world. In just two years the movement had taken root in over 50 nations, and was thought to have penetrated every U.S. town with a population of more than 3,000.

Because missionaries were some of the first to come, missions remain a fundamental part of the spiritual genetic code of the Pentecostal Movement, and one of its greatest strengths. Throughout the Scriptures it is seen that the power of God has always come in its greatest demonstrations where there was the greatest darkness. The first ones to carry the Pentecostal movement abroad were hardened, seasoned missionaries who greatly appreciated what they had been given. They used the power they had been given, and multitudes of men women and children were delivered from bondage. Soon missionary reports back to home churches read like a modern book of Acts, adding even more fuel to the fire of the movement at home.

When it was discovered that the greatest demonstrations of the Spirit's power usually came in the darkest, neediest places, it compelled many to go on mission trips just to witness the power of God. This added great strength and depth to the new movement, and kept it growing throughout the world. Pentecostal children grew up hearing of the testimonies of God's power from missionaries. Because such esteem was given to these missionaries, they often became the children's greatest heros. Emulating their heros, many of these children of the early Pentecostal pioneers grew up to be missionaries so that they could live close to such wonderful activities of the Spirit. Others became pastors and evangelists who founded new churches and ministries all across America. Many of them are now leaders of the great Pentecostal churches and denominations. Each of them is like a vast treasure houses filled with stories of the glory of God. They walked with Him and learned His ways. They learned to be hosts to the Holy Spirit. They grew up believing that the book of Acts was not just a history book, but a living guide for normal church life.

Many of their own stories read like a modern book of Acts as they earned their place as elders of the church.

We do not see in order to believe, but we believe in order to see. Because it is basic Pentecostal theology that God is the same today as He was yesterday, that He does everything today that He did in Scripture, true Pentecostals believe in His present working, and so they see it. Most Pentecostals will begin to wonder where they have gone wrong if they are not witnessing regular demonstrations of the power of God. To them it is blasphemy to think that God was an author who wrote just one book and then retired. They must have a living relationship with a *living* God, and so they do.

This was the experience at Azusa Street. Believers were in constant awe at the works of God in their midst. People forgot to eat or sleep, sometimes for days at a time, because they were so caught up in the presence of the Lord. Like the manna that came from heaven, every day they expected a fresh experience with the Lord. Faith built on faith until the humble little mission really had become a window of heaven.

A House of Prayer for All Nations

At any given time the Azusa Mission would be packed with such a diversity of people that some considered this almost as much of a marvel as the extraordinary miracles that were taking place. It began with a few black men and women in a little home group, but soon most of those who came were white. In one meeting over twenty nationalities were counted. Fine ladies could be found lying prostrate on the floor next to domestic servants and washer women. Prominent churchmen and high government officials sat next to hobos. No one seemed to care. They all had one thing in common—they came to receive the Holy Spirit of God.

A Father Tries to Kill His Children

Charles Parham visited Seymour, his former student, in the fall of 1906. He wanted to see for himself the great work that was already the talk of Christians around the world. Seymour was thrilled to have a visit from his mentor, and warmly welcomed him. However, Parham was deeply offended by what he saw. He thought that the various charismatic gifts were too openly demonstrated, and he was appalled by the way so many fell to the ground in apparent trances (one report described Azusa as sometimes resembling "a forest of fallen trees").

Seymour realized that some were faking the manifestations, and believed that these were tares sent by the devil to foul the field of wheat. Even so, he held to the biblical wisdom to let the wheat and tares grow up together. He knew that if he tried to root out the tares, the wheat would also be uprooted—if he stopped that which was not real, he would also quench the Spirit and the work that was real. He determined that the risk of having some problems was acceptable in view of the spiritual benefits at stake. He was right. When he later succumbed to the pressure and changed this policy, the revival quickly died.

Even more than the faking of experiences, Parham was appalled by the unusual social and racial integration. Parham admired the Ku Klux Klan, and especially objected to racial mixing or mingling during worship and at the altar. However, he did not believe this just out of racial pride, but because of a false doctrine. He believed the great sin of humanity that caused the judgment of the flood was racial mixing, and that Noah was chosen to survive because of his pedigree, being "without mixed blood." This is a tragic and diabolical misunderstanding of Scripture that has been the twisted theological basis upon which many racist groups, including the Nazis, have been built.

The Bible does say that Noah was chosen because "he was perfect in his generations" (see Genesis 6:9 KJV), or literally, "perfect in his genealogy," but this had nothing to do with the mixing of human races. The mixture that so offended the Lord was the mixture of the fallen angels with men which had produced the superhuman "nephilim" (see Genesis 6:4). This was a race that the Lord did not create, and threatened the destruction of men who He did create, which He also planned to redeem. This seems to have been Satan's attempt to pre-empt the "new creation" man that would be brought forth when the Lord gave His Spirit to men.

In contrast to Parham's philosophy, Seymour felt that an essential element of Christianity itself was a unity which saw beyond the barriers of race, color, gender, nation, class or status. This was a demonstration that God is no respecter of persons, and that all believers are truly one in Christ. To him, the Azusa Street Mission was becoming a taste of what true Christianity was meant to be, just as the first Pentecost saw the coming together of those from every nation.

Seymour's leadership of such a renewal marked by interracial equality, harmony and unity is even more remarkable when it is understood that this took place during the most severely segregated time in American history. It was also composed mostly of the two most embittered racial groups—the poor whites and poor blacks. When the revival spread, it was also most readily received in the Southern states where this conflict was then most prevalent.

This is another sign of true revival; the waters of God always flow to the lowest points, and He sends His light to the darkest places. A leading British clergyman, A. A. Boddy, wrote, "One of the most remarkable things

[about the revival] was that preachers of the Southern states were willing and eager to go over to those Negro people in Los Angeles and have fellowship with them." Frank Bartleman wrote, "The color line was washed away in the blood."

Charles Parham had been mightily used by God at times, but the seeds of deception from some of his doctrines were maturing at a time when the enemy could make the greatest use of them. This has been another tragic way in which history has continually repeated itself. Those who begin a movement will almost always persecute those who seek to take it further, or who are used to start another subsequent movement. One of the worst curses placed upon biblical Israel for her apostasy was that they would eat their own children. The apostasy of the church has brought this terrible curse upon herself in almost every generation. Spiritual fathers seem to inevitably try to devour their own spiritual children.

When Parham could not force his style of leadership upon the Azusa Street Mission, he denounced it, and started another rival mission at the fashionable Women's Christian Temperance Union Building. This was the first schism in the Pentecostal Movement. When this rival mission failed, he spent the rest of his life denouncing Seymour and the Azusa Street Revival. By this he sealed his own spiritual doom. He continually lost influence and followers until his death in 1929.

The Gift

The Pentecostal/Charismatic Movement began under the leadership of a black man, and with a small group of black people. They freely shared what they had been given, and were delighted when they saw the Spirit poured out on those from other races, especially whites. They felt that the Lord had given them the greatest gift, and they were thrilled that they were able to share it with their white brethren. That this great world-wide revival was a contribution from the black community has never been denied by white Pentecostals, but it is often forgotten.

Many of the white leaders who themselves went to Azusa Street to receive the baptism, remarkably still held to the prevalent segregationist beliefs of the times. They took the blessing back home to their all-white congregations in which no blacks were welcome. This was not true of all, but it was of most, and the entire Pentecostal Movement quickly developed into the white and black streams that still prevail today.

However, the separate black and white streams in this movement was not the way it began, and obviously was not the way that the Lord wanted it, but it is understandable. The spiritual battle that began to rage against the baptism in the Holy Spirit itself was probably the most fierce persecution that Christians in this nation have ever experienced. Until the Charismatic Renewal made speaking in tongues almost fashionable, the price for being a Pentecostal was very high. Caricatures of Pentecostals in newspapers across the country depicted them as anything from devil worshipers to lunatics. Employment was difficult, if not impossible, for anyone found to be Pentecostal. Their houses and their churches were often burned. The children of Pentecostals were ostracized, called "devil worshipers," and subjected to ruthless beatings by other children. Many had to flee from the homes and towns that they had grown up in.

Both the press and historians have turned a blind eye to this persecution against Pentecostals. It was, at times, as terrible and degrading as what African-Americans suffered

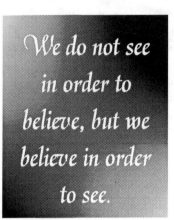

We do not see in order to believe, but we believe in order to see.

under segregation. For black Pentecostals it was a double jeopardy, as they were secluded from the white culture because of their race, and then from the black culture because of their religion. Just as the first Reformers risked all that they had so that later generations could enjoy religious freedom, two generations of Pentecostals paid the price for our freedom to know the Holy Spirit in our churches the way that we do today. They did it because they loved the Holy Spirit, and they counted knowing Him and allowing Him freedom in the church as more important than any freedom that the world could give them.

Because of this intense persecution against Pentecostals, to add to this a battle with the powerful forces of segregation and bigotry, was understandably more than many felt they could handle at the time. Military history teaches that it will almost always result in defeat to try to fight a two-front war, so the battle against racism in the church would have to wait for another generation. Even so, the Pentecostal Movement began with those from every race, creed and social position, in unity, seeking the Lord together. The power that was released to impact the world has never been as great as it was in those first years at Azusa when this unity existed. It is apparent that the Pentecostal/Charismatic movement, and indeed the church, will never come into its full potential until this unity is permanent. His house will be "a house of prayer for all nations" (Greek *ethnos*, or literally "ethnic races").

From the first Day of Pentecost, the Holy Spirit has proven that He will only come to the degree that we have unity. Like those who came to the Azusa Street Mission, we must want the Holy Spirit more than we want to hold on to our differences. Christianity was born as a multi-cultural entity, on the Day of Pentecost when men had gathered from "every nation." It was fitting that this is the way that the Holy Spirit came again at Azusa. In the little group at Antioch which sent out the first missionaries to the Gentiles, there was represented those from different races and social positions. When the Lord wants to do something truly great in the earth, this seems to be a dynamic that is required. In its most pure form the church will always be multi-cultural. That is why Paul had to resolutely confront Peter concerning his hypocrisy of not eating with the Gentiles. Racial equality before God is fundamental to the gospel.

It is debatable whether this multi-racial nature of the church was lost by the church because of her drift into apostasy, or whether it caused that drift. Regardless, it is the true state of the church that was born on the Day of Pentecost when the Holy Spirit first came to the church, and we will only be the true church to the degree to which we recover it. This is being realized by many church leaders today, and overcoming racism is now rightly a major thrust almost across the spectrum of Christianity. This is certainly one of the most positive signs of our times.

Where the Spirit Is, There Is Liberty

There is another aspect to Seymour's remarkable leadership at Azusa. It was his ability to discern and trust the Holy Spirit's leadership, and give Him the freedom that He requires, if we will know His fulness. In spite of almost constant pressure from world-renowned church leaders, who came from around the globe to impose what they perceived to be needed order and direction on the revival, for over two years Seymour held the course and allowed the Holy Spirit to move in His own, often mysterious, ways. Like Evan Roberts, who was at the same time leading the

great Welsh Revival, Seymour's greatest leadership quality was his ability to follow the Holy Spirit.

Seymour and Roberts both believed that the Holy Spirit required the freedom to move through whomever He chose, not just the leadership. They both resolved to allow anyone to be used by the Lord, even the most humble believers. This sometimes brought embarrassment, but more often it allowed the Holy Spirit to do marvelous things among them. If we really want the Holy Spirit in our midst, we must allow Him to be the leader. He is, after all, God.

God's Sovereignty Or The Free Will of Man

This has been one of the most ancient debates in the church. However, they are both true, and they are not in conflict with each other. Neither is either of these truths fifty percent of the truth. They are both one hundred percent true. God is utterly sovereign, and He has also, in His sovereignty, delegated authority to men that He will not even violate Himself.

Without freedom there could be no true worship or true obedience. That is why the Lord placed the Tree of Knowledge in the Garden. There could be no true obedience if there were not also the freedom to disobey. The Lord is the unquestioned Sovereign of the Universe, but when He delegates authority, He does not even violate it Himself. Otherwise we would never be able to rule and reign with Him. To rule requires both authority and responsibility. Therefore, even though He always knows what we need even before we ask Him, He always waits for us to ask.

For this reason, **"where the Spirit of the Lord is, there is liberty" (II Corinthians**

3:17). Liberty is required for true worship or true obedience. He has removed the veil into His presence for all, but we must seek Him. Therefore, we are all as close to God as we want to be. We are also as far from Him as we choose to be. If His manifest presence is not in our midst it is not because of Him, but because of our own choice. Many give lip service to wanting the Holy Spirit to lead their meetings, but really are not willing to give up their own programs, or trust Him in the way that He requires if He is to do this. Seymour was willing.

This kind of "hands off" leadership style has been a hallmark of most of the world's great revivals. However, even a cursory study of church history reveals that outside of revival it has seldom, if ever, worked. God simply moves in different ways at different times. In times of true revival there are usually dramatic and unique demonstrations of His sovereignty, and it is best to just stay out of His way. The rest of the time He seems to delight most in working with and through men. Even so, our goal should always be to submit our will to His, and always follow His leading. The more we can do this, the more He will usually manifest His wonderful presence.

As Vance Havner, one of the great revivalists of modern times, once observed, "Revival is like a sale at the department store. It is more dramatic, and gets more press, but the normal business of the store is the day to day merchandizing of products." Revivals are likewise much more spectacular, but they are not the normal business of the church. Much more has been accomplished for the overall advancement of the gospel by the day to day witnessing of faithful saints, and by the service of faithful pastors of local churches, who day by day fight on the front lines of the battle against darkness, than has ever been accomplished by a revival.

Revivals have sparked great spiritual advances, but they are sustained only by the day to day devotion of the saints. This is likewise the story of the Pentecostal/Charismatic Movement. Azusa was spectacular, as were other subsequent revivals and movements, but the real and substantial advance has come from a multitude of lesser known, but nevertheless faithful leaders and people.

The same is true in our personal lives. Spectacular spiritual experiences are wonderful, and can propel us to great heights of devotion and worship. Even so, the real strength of every Christian's life will usually be found in the degree of faithfulness to the disciplines of Bible study, prayer, fellowship and day to day witnessing.

In times of revival, there is also a dynamic, manifest presence of the Holy Spirit that makes deviations apparent to almost everyone, including those who make them. Needed corrections are therefore usually automatic. However, when we do not have this dynamic presence of the Lord that is found in revival, almost every vacuum of leadership will be quickly filled with the immature, the prideful, or the rebellious. The result of this will not be revival, but confusion, or worse.

It is very important that we do not "get the cart in front of the horse," in the leadership we use. Seymour could use the leadership style that he did *because* he had revival. If he had tried to use this style with the same number and types of people without the dynamic of revival present, he would have had worse than chaos—he would have had war! This has happened to many who have tried to exhibit revival type leadership without revival. The key is to be ready to step aside when the presence of the Lord does come.

Our goal should be to have such a manifest presence of the Lord in all of our meetings. However, the way to do this is not to just sit back and do nothing until He comes, but to faithfully press on to maturity by seeking to increasingly be sensitive to His leading. Occasionally the Lord catches us up in a spectacular manifestation of His presence, but usually leads us to higher ground like a father teaching his child to walk. He will help us to stand, and then back off so that we must walk to Him. As we learn to take a couple of steps, He backs further away so that we have to walk further. He is not just playing with us when He removes His manifest presence, He is teaching us to walk in the Spirit and to pursue Him. When we do not feel Him it is not a time to sit down, but to try to take more steps.

The New Testament epistles are basically the apostles' exhortations to leaders who were serving in times that were not dynamic revivals. They did not expect the Spirit to come every day like He did on the Day of Pentecost, so they went about doing the day to day work of the ministry. However, when He does decide to come in a dramatic way that ignites a revival, it's time to drop what we're doing and ride the wave for as far as it will take us.

Wisdom is to know when the Lord is telling us to go forth and take the land, or when He is telling us to stand and watch His salvation. There are times for each, and anytime we confuse them we will have problems. Seymour was called to lead in a revival. For a few years he exemplified the wisdom to just stay in prayer and let the Lord do the leading (he actually kept his head in a box during the meetings so that his prayer would not be distracted by all that was going on). However, the fierce persecution raised up against the movement soon pressured him into an increasingly protectionist stature. Gradually he allowed more and more control of the meetings to be taken over by a few leaders. Soon they were following a program for the meetings. Those who were witnesses said that just as gradually as this happened the Holy Spirit seemed to depart.

This explanation of how the revival at Azusa Street ended could be the case. However, it is also possible that it was simply time to move on, and that the Spirit was withdrawing His presence so that the people would go

forth. Just as the sale at a department store would lose its impact if it went on all of the time, it does not seem that the Lord ever intended for revivals to last forever in their initial form.

Even so, most revivals do end prematurely, or in a way that was not preferable, because of human mistakes. We should learn from these, but let us also not fall into the trap of wrongly worshiping revival. We can be as close to the Lord today as anyone ever has been, even in the midst of the greatest revivals.

Without question, the Azusa Street Revival was one of the greatest in all of church history. It can be argued that it has not yet ended, but has gone on in many different forms, and in many different places. It is right for us to give honor to whom honor is due, and William J. Seymour must be considered one of the greatest Christian leaders of all time.

The Greatest Miracle

At the height of the Azusa Street revival Seymour prophesied, "We are on the verge of the greatest miracle the world has ever seen." The miracle he was referring to was a true love and unity between races and creeds that he considered to be fundamental Christianity. He did not live to see the completion of his dream, but he fully expected the renewal to ultimately accomplish it. As the movement has continued in a number of different forms, it is still more than possible, it is probable that his dream will come true. When it does, William J. Seymour must be considered as one who sowed the seeds for this greatest miracle of all. Possibly more than any other man in church history, he promoted that which alone can bring it to pass, seeking the fulness of the Holy Spirit in our midst.

Above all things the Holy Spirit has come to testify of Jesus. He alone can truly convict us of our sins and lead us into all truth. When the Holy Spirit does manifest Himself in our midst, we do not see the world in shades of black and white; we only see the glory of the Son of God. He has been given to us to help us see as God sees. God does not look on the outward appearance, but on the heart. God does not just see us as we are now, but He sees us through the blood of His Son, which is to see us as we are to become—made in the likeness of Jesus. We must begin to see each other the same way.

Paul the apostle had said that **"tongues are for a sign" (I Corinthians 14:22),** and that sign seemed to have been given on the first Day of Pentecost. That day men from every nation heard the glories of God in their own language. This was the first time since the Tower of Babel and the scattering of men's languages that this had happened. The sign was that the church would be the anti-thesis of the Tower of Babel, where men were scattered from each other. In the church, we will all be regathered as one.

Even as fractured and divided as the Pentecostal Movement may presently be, it has the destiny and calling to help bring unity to the whole church. The fire still burns in the Pentecostal Movement. The fire will burn until all of the wood, hay and stubble has been consumed, and the gold, silver and precious stones have been purified. Each movement may be fashioned into a different stone, but the day is coming when we will all be fashioned together into one crown of glory.

The explosive spread of the movement begun at Azusa continued as long as the Holy Spirit was free to move as He willed, and the people sat before Him as one. As the revival drifted from these basics, they also drifted from the source of their power. Where the Spirit is Lord there must be liberty, and where He is Lord there will be unity. Before the Lord we all look the same. The blood of Jesus does wash away all color lines.

It is interesting to note that the very name Azusa was derived from an Indian word that means "blessed miracle." This was first noted by Father Juan Crespi in 1769, while on the Portola expedition to explore California. At that time Azusa referred to the site of an old Indian village south of present day Los Angeles in the San Gabriel canyon. There a young Indian girl named Coma Lee used to pray and fast for the healing of her people. She was gifted with healing power as she laid hands on the sick. After she prayed for a chief who was wonderfully healed, he gave her the name Azusa to commemorate his miracle of healing. For many years, Azusa continued her healing ministry while her fame spread all over southern California. During that time whenever there was suffering, people said, "Go to Azusa and be healed . . . go to Azusa." Maybe it is time for us to again go to Azusa and be healed of the many wounds that we have inflicted upon one another. ■

AUTHOR'S NOTE: In a future edition of *The Journal* there will be a second article on the Azusa Street revival from the perspective of Frank Bartleman's contribution to it. These will then be expanded and combined into a book that will be a much more comprehensive study of this important move of God.

When God Walked The Earth

Part IV

Rick Joyner

Zebedee was becoming increasingly concerned over his son John. He seemed to be despondent over Jesus not returning for him as He had promised. James, John's brother, felt otherwise.

He thought that John was prone to be overly idealistic, and that this disappointment would be good for him. John now worked with such frustration that it seemed as if every task was an enemy that needed to be punished. Zebedee decided that it had gone too far and he had to talk to him.

"My son. I know that you put so much trust in this Jesus, but we should not put such trust in any man. Only God is worthy of such trust. He alone will never disappoint us. He is the only One we should devote ourselves to in such a way. Even the greatest prophets, even Moses and Elijah, made mistakes. It is because we as a people have been so easily prone to follow after men that we are now suffering this terrible yoke of being under the Romans. We have only gotten what we have deserved for not determining to have no other King but Jehovah."

John did not even look up to acknowledge his father's words. They each hit him like a slap in the face, even though he believed that what he was saying was true. He just did not know what to do. The months that he had spent with John the Baptist had been the most wonderful of his life. They had been filled with continual wonder at the Lord's activity. The Baptist stirred hopes of a greater move of God than Israel had ever experienced. Never had he felt such hope, such expectation, such wonder. Now the disappointment seemed to be just as terrible as those times had been wonderful. Even so, this time at home had confirmed to him that he could never go back to a normal life again. Even so, now he did not know what he was going to do.

"Father, I agree with what you are saying. I know that I will somehow get beyond the disorientation I now feel. But I know that I must either return to the Baptist, or somehow find Jesus. I cannot blame Jesus for not keeping His word. Anyone can forget. Something may have come up that prevented Him from coming."

"I will go find Him!" John blurted out, throwing down the net he had been mending. This resolve was like a wind blowing away the fog from his mind. Suddenly he felt better. "I will seek for Jesus until I find Him! If I have to I will not even eat until I do, but I will find Him and not do anything else until I do," he continued with such force that it shocked his father and brother.

"Whenever you seek Me you will find Me," a voice cascaded down from the bank above them. All three of the men wheeled around to see who had spoken.

"Master!" John shouted, leaping up the bank in giant strides. "You came for me!"

"Did you doubt that I would?"

"Well, it has been so long," John mumbled.

"Did you doubt My word?" Jesus asked again.

John did not know what to say, so he did not say anything. Jesus did not say anything either, but continued to look straight at him. Finally, John almost whispered, "I'm sorry. I did begin to doubt, but I knew that you must have had a good reason not to have come."

"You will learn that you never have reason to doubt My word," Jesus replied, as He reached out to take John's hand and pull him to the top of the bank.

Jesus then turned and looked down upon Zebedee and James. Both had been watching the scene with the greatest interest. John quickly spoke up, "Father, brother, forgive me for not introducing you. This is Jesus, whom I have told you about."

"Yes," Zebedee replied, "Our son has told us much about you. Can we please offer you hospitality in our home?"

"Sir, My Father and I have always appreciated the hospitality We have received in your home, as well as in the home of your father. That is why I have come for your sons. They will honor My Father and Me, as you and your father have done, and they will help to build Us a house so that We may one day receive you and your father, and show you hospitality."

Zebedee obviously did not understand Him. "Sir, have you been here before?" he asked.

"Friend, it is hard for you to understand now, but you will later. You and your house have honored God by seeking to know His ways, and by teaching your sons to trust His word. He will now honor you by using your sons."

As He was talking, He reached out His hand to pull James to the top of the bank. James took His hand shyly. "Will you join us?" Jesus asked, gazing intently at James.

James was stunned. A flood of thoughts arose from his heart. He had never considered himself a spiritual person like his brother. He tried to live by the rules, and sincerely tried to do what was right, mostly to honor his father and mother, but had really never felt a desire to know about God. God seemed too ambiguous and hard to understand. He had felt a subtle and almost continuous guilt about this, but now it was more than that. For some reason, at this moment, he felt a deep shame that he had not wanted to know more about God. Somehow, the presence of Jesus magnified these feelings in him to the point that he felt that he would either have to run, or weep.

"Do not be ashamed. You are not different from other men; no man desires to know God. Many do want to honor Him, but few want to know Him, and even fewer want to be close to Him. But the Father wants to be close to men, and He wants to be close to you. He wants to use you to help bring men closer to Him."

Each word seemed to hit James like a hammer upon his breast. John and his father were even embarrassed as tears began to flow down James' face. They had never seen him this emotional before, and he had never felt that way before. He was truly sorry that he had not tried to know God. He was also more glad than he could ever remember being as he considered what Jesus had just said to him. He could not only get close to God, but he was sure that somehow the Lord was right now, somehow, asking him to!

"Master, please just tell me what I need to do."

"Follow Me."

"I do not know you, but I somehow know that you are true. I feel as if the Lord Himself is speaking through you. You not only know what I am thinking, you are somehow drawing my deepest thoughts out of my heart. I have never felt like this, and I do not do things rashly, but I know that I will follow you."

Zebedee watched the entire scene in stunned silence. How could such a brief encounter with a stranger have such an impact upon his son? And why was it that in spite of his astonishment, he was not feeling dismay, but peace? He knew that, even as crazy as it all seemed, it was also right.

Jesus then turned and looked at Zebedee. As He did Zebedee felt something that he had not felt since he was a young child. He called it "the joyful Presence." When he sat on the edge of the sea pondering the glory of all that God had made, he would begin to feel as if the Lord Himself would join him. Many times he had asked the Lord to show him His glory just as He had shown it to Moses. He was always afraid that the Lord would do it, but he had determined that, as frightening as it might be, it would be worth it. The feeling of the "wonderful Presence" that would often come upon him at such times was the greatest feeling he had ever had. He knew that if he were able to ever visibly see the Lord's glory, it would be ecstasy beyond anything that he could ever otherwise experience. As he had grown and taken on many responsibilities he had not returned to such times of reflection and joy in just pondering the Lord. Now, so abruptly, that same joy was all over him. He felt the "wonderful Presence."

"Master," Zebedee almost whispered. "I used to pray to see the glory of the Lord. I never did, but I know that I have felt His nearness. I feel Him now. Maybe it is not for me to see His glory, but if my sons go with you, I know that they too will know the joy of His presence. There is no greater joy for me now than for my sons to go with you. I know in my heart that you have been sent by God to visit our land. Our family prayer, which I have heard all of my life, and which they have heard all of theirs, is that our family would be used to bring honor to the great name of our God. Somehow, I know that you are here because of those prayers. I will miss my sons, but this is a great day for me. I thank the God of my fathers for hearing our prayers."

"Friend. Your prayer to see the glory of God has been answered. God also knows what it means to send His Son. You have given Him two, and He will reward you. He will reward you with the closeness to Him that you have desired all of your life."

"We will come to you again and enjoy the hospitality that you offered, but now we must depart. I have a purpose for which I cannot delay, and you have an old Friend who has missed the times that you used to have together."

Zebedee arose, climbed the small bank, and embraced each of his sons. As he turned to face Jesus he felt the great Presence with even more intensity. His eyes furrowed as he tried to hold back the flood of tears that were about to erupt. Jesus reached out and touched his shoulder, and then turned and departed. The little troop followed after him.

Zebedee watched them turn the corner. He felt sadness at the departure of his sons, but he also felt a great joy. He stepped back into the boat and pushed off. He was going to spend the night on the water. He had a Friend who he had not been with for a very long time, and he could not do anything else until he got alone with Him again. "I'm sorry that I ever grew up, and lost what I had with God then," Zebedee thought to himself. "I must become a child again. I must never again lose what I had then, and what I felt when Jesus came here today."

Simon and Andrew watched the encounter with Zebedee and his sons with amazement. Andrew was glad to see his friend John, but Simon had already started to feel a little possessive of Jesus. Even so, Simon was astonished by the whole encounter with Zebedee and his sons. He had to fight his own emotions as hard as he could to keep from crying with them. He had never even seen Zebedee before, but he began to feel a love for him as if he were his own father. He was even now sorry that they had to leave him so quickly.

For almost an hour the men walked on in a slightly awkward silence. Finally, Simon spoke up.

"Master. Where are we going?"

"We are going to the house of Israel," Jesus replied. "We will start in Galilee, and then we will move from place to place as the Father leads us. We must go to the whole house of Israel."

"But what will we be doing?" Andrew ventured.

"We will be doing more than you can now understand, even if I were to explain it to you. Even so, please ask Me what is on your heart to know. I want you to understand everything, but some things you just can't until you have experienced them."

This encouraged Simon and the others. Soon they were all trying to ask Him questions at once. Jesus stopped, raised His hand for silence, and then began to explain to them something that they had not asked, but which somehow appeased all of their other questions.

"My ultimate desire for you is that you understand as I do, and that you will do the works that I do. Therefore I will *do* and then *teach*. You must not be satisfied to just see My works, but you are called to understand them, and then to do them yourselves. After you grow in faith to do My works, you must teach others to do the same."

"Master, what works are you talking about? Are we going to be baptizing, like John? Or will you do something else?" John asked.

"Yes, we will at times baptize, but I am talking about other works. Tomorrow you will begin to see them."

Just hearing conversation after the group had walked so far in the awkward silence was a relief. Quickly, there was almost a buoyancy in the group. The uncomfortable feelings were displaced by a deep but sober joy. As the joy permeated the group, Simon's protectiveness toward Jesus was displaced by thankfulness that others had also joined them. He walked over to introduce himself to the sons of Zebedee. After a while longer, Jesus called for James to walk beside Him so that they could talk.

"The shame that you felt earlier, when you first saw Me, was the same guilt that Adam felt, which caused him to hide from God after his sin. All men are still hiding

The secret is to become wise before you get old.

H. J. Brown

You will find as you look back upon your life that the moments when you have really lived are the moments when you have done things in the spirit of love.

Henry Drummond

Sometimes we Christians, instead of being fishers of the lost, become critics of the saved; instead of casting nets, we cast stones; instead of extending helping hands, we point accusing fingers; rather than helping the hurting, we hurt the helpers.

Max Lucado

from Him. This shame has all men in bondage. Because of this, they do not want to see God, or hear Him."

James did not reply, but he immediately understood what Jesus was talking about. After a few moments, He continued:

"There are many ways in which men hide from God because of their shame. Many in Israel even hide from Him by zealously trying to serve Him, performing sacrifices and devoting themselves to religious activity. But they do not worship Him with this activity; they are worshiping their own works. They are, by this, putting their trust in their own works more than in Him. All who truly desire to serve God must do what you did. They must choose not to hide, but to come out into the light of My Father's Presence. You are called to be one of My evangelists, and that is your job—to help men come out of their hiding places to stand in the Presence of God."

"Sir. Turning to you, instead of away from you, was one of the hardest things I have ever done. I really do not even know how I was able to do it."

"You received help," Jesus replied. "No man can come to Me unless the Father helps them. No amount of human persuasion can release a man from the great bondage that shame has on his heart. That is why you must come to know the Holy Spirit, Who My Father will send to testify of Me to all He is calling. It was not just My words that persuaded you, but a knowledge that came to your heart that I was true. It is the Holy Spirit who makes My words living, and like sharp swords, able to cut the yokes that are upon the hearts of men. As My evangelist, you will be entrusted with the same Power in your words, which will testify of Me."

"Sir," James responded. "If I had not had the experience, I know that I could not understand what you are talking about.

Because of what I just experienced, I do understand. But I have never thought of anything like this before."

"And neither has anyone else. This is why I must *do* and then *teach*. I have not come to work in the same way that any man has worked before. My works are from above, and men who are from the earth cannot understand them until they have been helped by the Holy Spirit. The ways of God are different than men's ways. He does not think like men, but religious men believe that He thinks just like they do. Therefore, religious men are the most difficult men for the Holy Spirit to help. It was much easier for you to understand and come to Me because you were not a religious man."

James was really surprised by this statement. "I always thought that religious men were the closest to God."

"No. Really you did not think that. Deep in your heart you knew that was not the way to God. Deep in your heart you knew that the Lord was not concerned about rituals and sacrifices. In your heart, you felt that God must be above all of that, and you were right."

"Then why are so many of our holy men so zealous for these rituals?" James asked, still troubled by the thought that these men were not serving God, though they were devoting their lives to this service.

"One act of kindness means more to God than a lifetime of performing rituals. Rituals can have their place if they are used to stir men to love, but they are enemies of truth when they are used to take the place of love," Jesus replied, turning and saying it loud enough for the rest to hear. "Rituals can be one of the thickest cloaks that men will use to try to hide from God. I have come to strip away this cloak so that men can come out of hiding, walk in truth, and walk with the Lord again just as Adam did before the fall."

WHEN GOD WALKED THE EARTH IV

"You are now with Me because you made the decision not to hide from God or yourself. You did this because the Holy Spirit gave you peace in your heart, and the knowledge that I am true. The Holy Spirit is a Helper—He does not force Himself upon men. Only when a man chooses to come out of hiding into His light can He help them. He moves upon them to draw, but He does not push. Religious men are the most resistant to His help, because they trust in their own righteousness, which they use to cover up their shame. For a man to get free, he must allow the shame to be exposed, acknowledge it, and be willing to come into the light in order to be set free. It is for this reason that the publicans and harlots will come to God before those who consider themselves righteous."

James was even more surprised by this statement. "Do you mean that publicans and harlots can come to God?"

"Yes," Jesus replied. "They are all loved by the Father. He loves all men, even the self-righteous, even though they are much harder for Him to reach."

"Please forgive me if I am presumptuous, but You almost make it sound as if the publicans and sinners are closer to God, and that the religious ones are the furthest from Him. I understand what you are saying about how rituals are misused, but it is hard to believe that those who give themselves to lives of sin can more easily come to God," James almost whispered, as if he did not want anyone else to hear him.

"It is a hard saying, but it is true," Jesus replied. "Many of the worst sinners will come to Me before those who appear to be the most religious and upstanding citizens. Pride caused the devil to fall, and has caused the fall of almost everyone since. Pride is to think that you do not need God. Pride is to think that you could ever be righteous or acceptable on your own merit. That is what

caused Satan to fall from grace; he is actually the most religious being in the creation. That is why he usually appears as if he were an angel of light. Those who follow him the closest try to appear the same, and are usually deceived into thinking that they have more light than anyone else. Only the humble will acknowledge their shame instead of trying to cover it up. Only the humble will acknowledge that they are in the darkness and need the light. That is why Isaiah said:

"Who is blind but My servant, or so deaf as My messenger whom I send? Who is so blind as he that is at peace with Me, or so blind as the servant of the LORD?

"You have seen many things, but you do not observe them; your ears are open, but none hears.

"The LORD was pleased for His righteousness' sake to make the law great and glorious.

"But this is a people plundered and despoiled; all of them are trapped in caves, or are hidden away in prisons; they have become a prey with none to deliver them, and a spoil, with none to say, 'Give them back!'

"Who among you will give ear to this? Who will give heed and listen hereafter?" (Isaiah 42:19-23).

"Satan fell because he allowed pride to enter his heart. Therefore God will only give His grace to the humble. The Law was great and glorious, but it could only help those who would humble themselves before it. When men see the Law, and exalt themselves before it, this is the greatest form of pride, and they will use it for an even greater evil. They will use it to plunder their brothers with it, just as was spoken through Isaiah."

The group walked along for a few minutes. James was in deep thought. This was so new to him. He had respected the most those whom Jesus said were probably the furthest from God. He had respected the least those whom He said were the closest. As if knowing His thoughts, Jesus continued:

"It is not right to think that the ways of the publicans and sinners are closest to God. They are not. However, they will more easily come to Him because they know that they are in darkness, and they will more quickly humble themselves to acknowledge their need for help. The self-righteous will be offended by even the suggestion that they need help. Because God has given to man the freedom to choose, man must choose to accept His help. He will only do this to the degree that he knows how badly he needs help.

"It was when Lucifer began to think that the light and power that he had came from himself that he turned from God to serve himself. Men who follow in his ways feel the same. This was the first sin, and it is the most difficult to free men of. To help men, the Holy Spirit will reveal to them their shame, illuminating their sin. It is at that point that they must choose to either receive My help, as you did, or go even deeper into hiding from My presence. Those who go deeper into hiding, whether it is by covering themselves with sin, or with the Law, they will fight the light with a greater ferocity, thinking that the light that threatens them is actually darkness. They know in their hearts that this is not true, but those who go this way have ceased to listen to their heart long ago.

"Earlier, you understood your sin, how you had tried to live by the rules, but how you did not do this for God, but for yourself. You confronted this and decided to repent, to turn to Me and follow Me. This was the most important choice that you have ever made, or ever will make. Even so, there are other areas of your life that are still hidden from God, which will be exposed as we walk together, and you will have to make the same choice each time. When you see darkness in your own heart, do not try to hide it. If you do you will not hide you will always be set free. Your life will be filled with both more freedom and more joy. Do not run from me, but to Me. I will never be surprised or shocked by what is in your heart, because I have already seen it. I will never condemn you; I have come to set you free.

"When you are free, you must set others free with the same freedom that you have received. Never take pride in your freedom, or look down upon those who are not yet free, even the self-righteous. The Father loves all men, even those who resist Him. When He saw the sins of this world, He did not condemn it; it was already condemned. He sent Me to save the world. I am here to proclaim liberty to the captives, and to be a light to those who have hidden in darkness. I will receive any who will come out of the darkness into My light. It hurts to have the darkness that you have been hiding in stripped away by the light, but it is the path of freedom, and after you are delivered the pain will have been worth it. You are with Me to help men come out of hiding, to remove that with which they have tried to cover themselves, so that they can stand before Me with nothing between us. Then I will cover their nakedness with light.

"When you feel exposed, do not hide, but come to Me. The more you learn that you can trust Me, the more you will be willing to be exposed to My light. Trust cannot be forced. We must therefore allow men to walk by faith, not by force. True faith begins by coming out of hiding to be exposed to the light. True faith is to be willing to be naked, exposed, and vulnerable, knowing that I have not come to hurt you, but to help you. Faith in My intentions, and My power to help, is the most powerful force in the creation. It is more powerful than the pride of men or devils, and it will crush their strongholds over men.

"You and this little group are the beginning of a great march of faith. It will be a long march, but men will come to believe Me. As they do, and they come out of hiding, the power of the light will grow in them. The release of this power will enable many others to know that they, too, can trust Me and come out of hiding. This power will grow in those who come to Me, until one day, they are used to do greater exploits than have ever been done on this earth."

"Master, do you mean greater miracles?" Simon blurted out, who had been trying to catch every word of the conversation between James and Jesus.

"Yes, I mean greater miracles. The greatest miracles that God has done upon the earth have not even required the lifting of His little finger. Just as He has parted seas, He will one day part mountains, because of the prayers of faith that come from little children who trust Him."

Michael and the captains who stood with him were also listening to all that Jesus was saying, as were the thousands of angels who stood all around them. As a peaceful silence had come upon the little group that walked along the dusty road with Jesus, one of the captains spoke up:

"I have been here since the devil was allowed to tempt the first man and woman, but I have never understood the great evil that lives in men or the fallen angels like I do now. What Satan tried to tell us was weakness is really the source of our strength. He tried to cause us to rebel by enticing us to come to know ourselves, and live by what he calls "the great light that is within each of us." I have often been concerned that I never felt that there was a great light within me, but that I only had what the Father had given me. I have not understood why it seemed that the more I felt this way, that I was lacking in great light and power within me, the more I felt dependent on the Father, the higher I was promoted. Now I see that this is the truth that upholds the creation—we only have what we have been given. The more that we know that all power and light comes from the Father, the more that we can be trusted with power and authority."

"That is why men will one day even judge us," Michael offered. "Those who have fallen into such depravity and darkness, who are so weak and blind, will know even more deeply their dependence on the Father. Therefore He will trust them with more authority, because they will know, even more deeply, that they cannot trust in themselves.

"Yes, and that is why the Son has become one of them—to help them to come out of hiding and into the light of God once again. Now we are learning more about our God every day than we have learned since the beginning. How great is the blessing that we have received, to be here and able to see these things!

"How blessed are these men who come to Him, who hear His words and behold the glory of His ways. To behold this has truly been worth all of the battles. All of the darkness that our enemy has brought into the creation only makes the glory of our God much brighter. He is worthy, He who is the Source of all authority and power, glory and dominion! How great and wonderful are these times," Michael continued.

All of the angels replied, "Amen!" ∎

New Music Releases

from EagleStar Productions

These are our first "live" albums, and they really do capture some of the most anointed worship we have experienced at our conferences.

To Order Call 1-800-542-0278 — CREDIT CARD ORDERS ONLY

Worship

with Leonard Jones & Matthew Donovan

Recorded live at the MorningStar Conference, "Worship & Warfare, The Heart of David." This album contains some of our most popular new songs. Retail price: Cassette $10.95/CD $15.95

Cassette   ES6-003   Our Price $10.00
CD   ES6-004   Our Price $14.00

oh, jah! • dance into the land • mighty god • creator of the universe • god of peace • rise in me

&

Warfare

with Don Potter

There is a militancy sweeping the church as she receives her marching orders from the Spirit to take back that which has been stolen. You will feel the cadence in this album. Retail price: Cassette $10.95/CD $15.95

Cassette ES6-005 Our Price $10.00
CD ES6-006 Our Price $14.00

i have decided • our god is holy • repentance • nacah [accepted]

Directory

CHURCHES

Belmont Church
Jackie Lusk, Assist. to Sr. Associate Pastor
68 Music Square East, Nashville, TN 37203-4041
Don Finto, Pastor; Stephen Mansfield, Sr Asst Pastor
(615) 256-2123 / (615) 259-9184 fax

The Meeting Place
A New Testament Church
Gaffney, SC 29341
Steve Osborn (864) 488-1229
Lane Carter (864) 489-6262

The Missionary Church International
A Convention of Churches
Benjamin H. Covington, Bishop
P.O. Box 1761, Columbia, SC 29202
(803) 799-0502 / (803) 254-7446 fax

New Dawn Community Church
Randal L. Cutter, Pastor
11030 Wiles Road, Coral Springs, FL 33076
(954) 753-7729 / (954) 345-2562 fax

Northside Church of Atlanta
Marc Lawson, Sr. Pastor
11800 Wills Road, Suite 150, Alpharetta, GA 30201
(770) 667-3778 / (770) 667-3820 fax /
nca@mindspring.com e-mail

Restoration Fellowship Church
David Hickey, Pastor
20409 CR 4118, Lindale, TX 75771
(903) 882-7496

Outside U.S.
Stockholm Vineyard
Gunnar Rydin
Ekensbergsv. 115
171 41 Solna, Sweden
+46-8-29 35 33 / +46-8-29 52 62 fax

CHURCH NETWORKS

The Missionary Church International
(with IRS Group Exemption Status)
Benjamin H. Covington, Bishop
P.O. Box 1761, Columbia, SC 29202
(803) 799-0502 / (803) 254-7446 fax

COUNSELING

Christian Counseling Services
Restoration Life Ministries, Inc.
Ray Kiertekles, A, Ministry Director
6045 Barfield Road, Suite 119, Atlanta, GA 30328
(404) 252-4656 / (404) 252-2343 fax

Listening Prayer Ministries
Dave & Linda Olson
2624 Wind River Rd., El Cajon, CA 92019
(619) 447-9458

Marriage Counseling
Dr. Sandra Joy Kellogg-Gray
3915 Old Lee Hwy, Suite 23-B, Fairfax, VA 22030
(703) 691-1933

CREATIVE

International Arts Mandate
David Traylor, Arts Counselor
P.O. Box 180, Kaneohe, Hawaii 96744-0180
(808) 247-2460 phone & fax

FINANCIAL SERVICES

Investment & Brokerage Services
Smith Barney, Inc.
Duncan Hill, First Vice Pres., Financial Cons.
237 West Main Street, Bozeman, MT 59715-4646
(406) 586-1776 / (800) 423-6206 / (406) 586-8694 fax

Certified Factoring Specialist
Peterson Funding Services
Paul W. Peterson
13204 E. 15th Ave., Spokane, WA 99216
(509) 922-3707 phone & fax / (800) 805-9960
"We buy accounts receivable nationwide."

Certified Public Accountant
Gary E. Cox, CPA
3098 Griggsview Ct., Columbus, OH 43221-4600
(614) 771-7536 / (614) 771-8638 fax

<u>Pinecrest Bible Training Center</u>

offers programs for one to three years of study. The Pinecrest program of study emphasizes a devotional relationship with the Lord, and is for those who want to set aside a special time of their lives to seek the Lord for a greater understanding of His Word and His Ways. Dormitories and trailers are available for students on campus. Costs are very reasonable. For more information or to request a catalog, please write, **The Registrar, Pinecrest Bible Training Center, Salisbury Center, New York 13454-9998** or call 315-429-8521.

THE BANNER is a quarterly publication of *Pinecrest Bible Training Center* and contains some of the most outstanding devotional articles available today. Included are articles from the writings and messages of *Wade Taylor, Walter Beuttler, John W. Follette, Seeley D. Kinne* and others. **THE BANNER** is edited by Wade Taylor and focuses on those topics which pertain to the Christian's devotional life and spiritual maturity. **THE BANNER** is available for a Freewill Offering simply by sending your request to **THE BANNER—Subscriptions, P.O. Box 320, Salisbury Center, New York 13454-9998** or call **315-429-8521**.

Call for information on Pinecrest Conferences: 315-429-8521

Directory

Certified Public Accountant
Barbara M. Holmes, CPA, CFP
420 Middle Highway, Barrington, RI 02806
(401) 247-2634 / (401) 247-0787 fax

Bi-Weekly Mortgage Program
ABBA Solutions Company
William Ginn, President
P.O. Box 477, Lake Jackson, TX 77566
(409) 297-4933 / (409) 297-1580 / (409) 297-5948 fax
"Not a refinancing plan."

MINISTRIES

Apocalyptic Ministries
Evangelistic Literature
Bruce E. Baker
P.O. Box 40, Wilmore, KY 40390
(606) 858-3148

Ascension Fellowships International
Sidney O. Stetson, General Secretary
10009 Branchview Ln., Knoxville, TN 37932
(423) 531-3838 / (423) 694-4226 fax

Calvary Commission, Inc.
**Short-Term Missions, Church Planting,
Prison Ministry, Missions Training**
P.O. Box 100, Lindale, TX 75771
(903) 882-5501 / (903) 882-7282 fax

Christ Encounter Ministry, Inc.
**Norman David Tracy and Donna Tracy,
Directors**
12250 Quail Mountain Rd., Tehachapi, CA 93561
(805) 822-7078

David Roch Growth Ministries
Prophetic Ministry
66080 - 29 Ave. NE
Calgary, AB, Canada, T1Y 3W5
(403) 293-7150 / (403) 280-6894 fax

Firestarter Ministries International
Mike & Becky Chaille
P.O. Box 242268, Charlotte, NC 28224
(704) 525-3880 / (800) 772-1899 (PIN # 85306)

Fulness Ministries International
Dr. Jimmy L. Brookins
3301 Riverside Drive, Coral Springs, FL 33065
(305) 752-4343 / (305) 752-4359

The Holy Way
Discipleship Training & Seminars
Edwin Stube, Executive Director
827 West Cross St., Baltimore, MD 21230-2501
(410) 752-1425

Jerusalem House of Prayer for All Nations
Tom Hess
P.O. Box 31393, Jerusalem 91313 Israel
972-2-274-126 / 972-2-894-239 fax

Jubilee Fellowship
Greater Ft. Lauderdale/Miami
Dale Moore, Pastor
P.O. Box 849221, Pembroke Pines, FL 33084
(954) 846-1002 / (954) 845-9735 fax
jubileef@netrus.net (e-mail)

The Master's Place Ministries
Prophetic/Teaching; offering credentials & monthly
newsletter
Bruce Hampton, Founder/Overseer
5160 N. Five Mile Rd., Hope, MI 48628
(517) 689-5713

Prophetic Interpretations
Dream & Vision Interpretations
Libby Magnello
5400 Parker Henderson,#298, Ft. Worth, TX 76119

Shepherd's Heart, Inc.
Dr. Harold and Ann Hammond
10875 Main Street, Suite 102, Fairfax, VA 22030
(703) 385-4833

TNT Evangelistic Association, Inc.
Ron Wallace
110 N.W. 207th Way, Pembroke Pines, FL 33029
(954) 437-7852 / (954) 437-7283 fax

Weiner Ministries International, Inc.
P.O. Box 1799, Gainesville, FL 32602
(904) 375-4455 / (904) 332-0080 fax

Daughters of the Lion Women's Prophetic Conference

with Mahesh and Bonnie Chavda

OCTOBER 24-26, 1996, CHARLOTTE, NC

featuring Mahesh Chavda, Bonnie Chavda, Patricia Bailey, and Robert Stearns-Worship Leader

- ◆ Personal Prophetic Ministry and Prayer for Healing
- ◆ Laying on of Hands for Commissioning
- ◆ Training in Spiritual Warfare and Prayer
- ◆ Worship and Special Music

Call 1-800-730-MCMI to register today by credit card,

or call 1-704-543-7272 for more information.

"Equipping Women to Take Their Place of Destiny in our Generation"

MEN ARE WELCOME!!!

Testimony: Julie writes: "The Daughters of the Lion Conference has totally changed our family. On Friday, Bonnie led us to shout to the Lord the names of our family members. I lifted my dad before the Lord. God totally changed him, and he rededicated his life to the Lord!" David writes: "I did not feel out of place at this "women's conference." There was ministry for the men that fit in with all the other ministry. I encourage men to bring their wives. Men, you will never be the same." ~David and Julie, FL

Directory

MINISTRY SCHOOLS

Grace Training Center
Mike Bickle, Director; Dr. Sam Storms, President
A Ministry of Metro Vineyard Fellowship
11610 Grandview Rd., Kansas City, MO 64137
(816) 765-4282 / (816) 767-1455 fax

I.M.I. Bible College & Seminary
Accredited Home Study & Extension Centers
Dr. M. A. Bruno, Vice Chancellor
P.O. Box 2107, Vista, CA 92085-2107
(619) 471-9390, 727-3998

Vision Christian College & International University
Stan E. DeKoven, Ph.D., President
Start a College in your church or achieve your degree.
940 Montecito Way, Ramona, CA 92065
(619) 789-4700 / (800) 9-VISION

MISSIONS

Your Missionary Outreach of The Missionary Church International
(with IRS Group Exemption Status)
Benjamin H. Covington, Bishop
P.O. Box 1761, Columbia, SC 29202
(803) 799-0502 / (803) 254-7446 fax

MUSIC MINISTRIES

John G. Elliott Ministries
Concerts & seminars
Galestorm Productions
P.O. Box 160777, Nashville, TN 37216-0777
(615) 227-0209 / (615) 228-7007 fax

NETWORKS

Youth Of All Nations
Networking Youth City to City, Philadelphia Base
Kent & Joy McCuen
22 Harding Ave., Hatboro, PA 19040
(215) 675-6134

PUBLISHING

Maranatha Publications, Inc.
P.O. Box 1799, Gainesville, FL 32602
(904) 375-6000 phone & fax

REAL ESTATE

Georgia:
Joe Davis
RE/Max Town Center
(800) 484-8388 / pin: 1996

MISCELLANEOUS SERVICES & PRODUCTS

Boarding Stables & Feed Store
Zion Farms Stables
2979 Big Texas Valley Rd. NW, Rome, GA 30165
(706) 232-3800

Computer Software
Hermeneutika BibleWorks for Windows
Mark Rice
P.O. Box 2200, Big Fork, MT 59911-2200
(406) 837-2244 / (406) 837-4433 fax

Health & Nutrition
Jeff Vietmeier
Super Blue Green™ Algae Products
For a FREE audio information tape, call or write:
P.O. Box 470992, Charlotte, NC 28247
1-800-338-5505 or (704) 650-4370 Independent
Distributor 98581

SAVE, Inc.
Survivability & Vulnerability Engineering
Dr. Norman J. Rudie
843 San Juan Lane, Placentia, CA 92670
(714) 524-5231 phone & fax

Tape Supplies
Record Life Tape Supplies
David Roch
Box 54053 Village Square PO
Calgary, AB, Canada, T1Y 6S6
(403) 293-7150 / (403) 280-6894 fax

Veterinarian Services
Dr. Roger L. DeHaan, DVM, MTS
A Holistic "2nd Opinion" Veterinarian
RR 1, Box 47A, Frazee, MN 56544
(218) 846-9112 phone consultations
"Natural Pet Care" book available ($10.95)

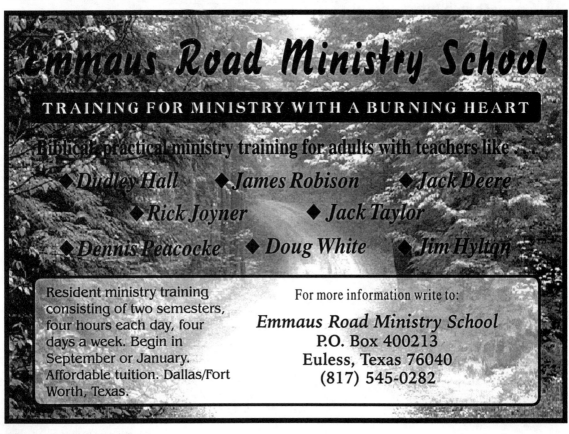

Directory
MorningStar Fellowship of Ministries

The MorningStar Fellowship of Ministries (MFM) was founded to serve three basic parts of the overall vision of *MorningStar*. First, is the equipping, oversight and support of ministries related to *MorningStar*. Second, is to use the relationship that *MorningStar* has with many different parts of the body of Christ to promote interchange, understanding and friendship between them. The third is for the mobilizing of spiritual forces for the sake of the gospel. Current members of MFM are listed below. For more information or an application please call our office at (704) 542-9880.

North

Bruce Hampton, Overseer
The Master's Place Ministries
5160 N Five Mile Rd., Hope, MI 48628
(517) 689-5713 phone & fax

Ted Moyer
V C F
P.O. Box 555, Westbend, WI 53095
(414) 626-3340 / (414) 338-2298 fax

Marc Tarr, Pastor
Calvary Worship Center
RR2 Box 84, Wheaton, MN 56296
(612) 563-4059

North East

John W. Connor
6 Summer St., Winthrop, ME 04364
(207) 377-2015

Tom Dobrient, Pastor
Cape Cod Christian Center
456 Phinney's Lane, Centerville, MA 02632
(508)771-0244

David Fenton, Pastor of Youth
Abide In The Vine Fellowship
1277 Taylor Rd., Owego, NY 13827
(607) 687-3426 / (607) 687-0043 fax

Vincent G. Gallagher, M.A.
Sr. Pastor, Mercy Christian Fellowship
314 Grandview Circle, Honey Brook, PA 19344
(610) 273-9194 phone & fax
vinny@chesco.com (E-mail)

Tom Hardiman, Pastor
LifeSpring Church
20 Dewberry Dr., Hamilton Twp, NJ 08610
(609) 581-8256 phone & fax

Fred Hoover, Pastor
Abide In The Vine Fellowship
1277 Taylor Rd., Owego, NY 13827
(607) 687-3426 / (607) 687-0043 fax

Rev. David Kyler, Retired Pastor
First Lutheran Church
223 S 2nd Street, Philipsburg, PA 16866
(814) 342-2433

Kay Lenear
3717 Washington Blvd., University Heights, OH 44118
(216) 321-9123 / (216) 371-1628 fax

John Metcalfe
4605 Olden Ct., Bowie MD 20715
(410) 721-1619 / jmet@tccs.com e-mail

Kent & Joy McCuen
Prayer Networking
22 Harding Ave., Hatboro, PA 19040
(215) 675-6134

Tom McDonald
334 Main Street, Owego, NY 13827
(607) 687-5971

Ozzie Ostrow
1531 Fairview Ave., Langhorne, PA 19047

John Price
P.O. Box 294, New Gretna, NJ 08224
(609) 294-1489 / (609) 294-1301 fax

Mike Quinn
263 Hoffman St., Franklin Square, NY 11010
(516) 437-4761 / (516) 354-6145 fax

Diane Scalchunes
12 Anchor Way, Port Washington, NY 11050
(516) 883-5036 / (516) 944-6879 fax

Wade E. Taylor, Director
Pinecrest Bible Training Center
P.O. Box 320, Salisbury Center, NY 13454
(315) 429-8521 / (315) 429-3354 fax

Gary Wallin, Pastor
Restoration Chistian Fellowship
19 Lansing Lane, East Northport, NY 11731
(516) 368-8909

Directory

MorningStar Fellowship of Ministries

East

Greg Booth
918 7th St., Huntington, WV 25701
(304) 525-6470 / (304) 529-6472 fax
(304) 529-6471 business

David Coleman, Pastor
Harvest Worship Center
PO Box 485, Patrick Springs, VA 24133
(540) 694-4639/ (540) 694-4933

Rev. Jerry Leach, Exec. Director
CrossOver Ministries
P.O. Box 23744, Lexington, KY 40523
(606) 277-4941 / (606) 278-9721 fax

AT Snoots
PO Box 456, Patrick Springs, VA 24133
(540) 694-4639/ (540) 694-4933

Barbara Watson, Co-Director
CrossOver Ministries
P.O. Box 23744, Lexington, KY 40523
(606) 277-4941 / (606) 278-9721 fax

Jerry & Ruthie Wickline, Pastors
Prophetic Family Ministry
Rt. 1, Box 58, Fayetteville, WV 25840
(304) 574-3948

South East

Joni Ames
P.O. Box 7188, Charlotte, NC 28241
(704) 583-0089

Mike & Becky Chaille
FireStarter Ministries International
P.O. Box 242268, Charlotte, NC 28224
(704) 525-3880 or (800) 772-1899 (Pin 85306)

Rick Compton
MorningStar Ministries
16000 Lancaster Hwy., Charlotte, NC 28277
(704) 542-0278/ (704) 542-0280 fax

Rainbow L. Cowan
15948 Lancaster Hwy., Charlotte, NC 28277
(704) 542-9880 / (704) 542-5763 fax

Aaron Evans
Joseph's Journeys
P.O. Box 472583, Charlotte, NC 28248
(704) 338-9385 / (704) 339-0631 fax

John Holcomb
MorningStar Ministries
12460-201 Sabal Park Dr., Pineville, NC 28134
(704) 523-6474 / (704) 523-5856 fax

Steve Lappin
2014 Cardinal Loop, Stanley, NC 28164
(704)822-2412

Mike Littlejohn
MorningStar Ministries
16000 Lancaster Hwy., Charlotte, NC 28277
(704) 542-0278/ (704) 542-0280

Leonard Jones
Eagle Star Productions
16000 Lancaster Hwy., Charlotte, NC 28277
(704) 542-0278 / (704) 542-0280 fax

Rick Joyner
MorningStar Ministries
16000 Lancaster Hwy., Charlotte, NC 28277
(704) 542-9880 / (704) 542-5763 fax

Scott MacLeod
Provision/The Foundry
296 Grangerview Circle, Franklin, TN 37064
(615) 791-1181 / (615) 831-3135
"Provision" phone & fax

Michael McBane
8010 Ridge Rd., Frederick, MD 21702
(301) 371-6595

Robin McMillan, Pastor
Cornerstone Church
P.O. Box 456, Pineville, NC 28134
(704) 889-4673 / (704) 889-4672 fax

Bill Perry
5000 Poplar Glen Dr, Matthews, NC 28105
(704) 821-7765

Don Potter
1860 JM Goodman Rd, Adams, TN 37010

Carey & Suzanne Ramsey
Lovingkindness Ministry
3240 Timberwolf Ave., High Point, NC 27265
(910) 886-1276

Dennis Rippy
MorningStar Ministries
16000 Lancaster Hwy, Charlotte, NC 28277
(704) 542-0278 / (704) 542-0280 fax

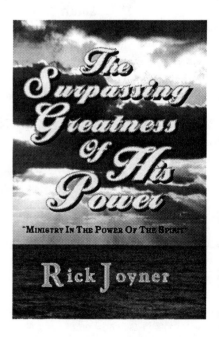

Directory
MorningStar Fellowship of Ministries

Don Robertson, Evangelist
D.R.E.A.M. Ministries
6015 Deveron St., Charlotte, NC 28211
(704) 442-1417 phone & fax

Craig Schaub, Pastor
Spirit of Life Church
3646 Murfressboro Rd., Antioch, TN 37013
(615) 641-5433 / (615) 641-5614 fax

Steve Thompson
MorningStar Ministries
16000 Lancaster Hwy., Charlotte, NC 28277
(704) 542-9880 / (704) 542-5763 fax

John & Fran Tullar
P.O. Box 1687, Etowah, NC 28729
(704) 877-4716

Robert & Kathy Whitlow
6700 Providence Rd., Charlotte, NC 28226
(704) 442-2137 / (704) 278-0582 fax

Don Wood
P.O. Box 1539, Hickory, NC 28603
(704) 261-0633 / (704) 327-9198 fax

Duane & Karah Young
New Beginnings School of the Spirit
P. O. Box 403, Pineville, NC 28134
(704) 543-5437

South

Miles Wylie Albright
Day's Dawn Ministries
245 C.R. 1595, Baileyton, AL 35019
(205) 796-2333

Linda Buchelt
Levite School of Worship
5637 Lakeland Highlands Rd., Lakeland, FL 33813
(941) 648-0779 / (941) 859-1121 fax

Steve Christmas
404 Cumberland Ave., Ocoee, FL 34761
(407) 656-5675

Paul Costa, Pastor
Love Covenant Fellowship
5425 Sunrise Dr, Birmingham, AL 35242
(205) 995-0468

Randal Cutter, Pastor
New Dawn Community Church
11030 Wiles Road, Coral Springs, FL 33076
(954) 753-7687 / (954) 345-2562 fax

Paul Davis, Pastor
Church of the Master
2065 McDade Rd., Hephzibah, GA 30815
(706) 733-4105 / (706) 785-4788 fax

Wendell Hollingsworth, Pastor
Abundant Grace Fellowship
102 Lynne Marie Dr., Thomasville, GA 31792
(912) 228-4019/ (912) 228-6721 fax

Annie Moore
2110 Longleaf Tr., Birmingham, AL 53243
(205) 978-5392/same fax number

Tom Norman
917 Eldorado Dr., Dothan, AL 36303
(334) 793-4095

Paul O'Higgins
Reconciliation Outreach, Inc.
P.O. Box 2778, Stuart, FL 34995
(407) 283-6920

Brigid Reickenback
1746 Yancey Ave., Montgomery, AL 36017
(334) 265-5491 / (334) 262-7842 fax

Ron Wallace
TNT Evangelistic Association
110 NW 207 Way, Pembroke Pines, FL 33029
(954) 437-7852 / (954) 437-7283 fax

David White, Pastor
Calvary Baptist Church
1309 Church St., Columbia, MS 39429
(601) 736-6336 / (601) 736-9456 fax

Mid-West

Michael Banes, Pastor
BYKOTA Church
403 E. 14th, Carthage, MO 64836
(417) 358-3991 / (417) 358-7876 fax
(417) 358-0714 home

Bill Ebert
16600 E Newton Pl., Tulsa, OK 74116
(918) 835-6700 / (918) 834-7218 fax

Doug Kimball
P.O. Box 473, Galveston, IN 46932
(219) 699-6184 / (317) 451-8493 fax
DTKIMBAL@MAIL.DELCOELECT.COM(e-mail)

Flo Rennaker
408 North Adams, Marion, IN 46952
(317) 644-1432

Directory
MorningStar Fellowship of Ministries

Mr. Kim Terrell
1337 Ticonderoga Dr., Ft. Collins, CO 80525
(970) 204-1453

West

Mr. Kim Andersson, Pastor
Christ the Rock Fellowship
P.O. Box 990971, Redding, CA 96099
(916) 222-6496

Fred Brason, Pastor
Coastlands Christian Fellowship
13866 Country Creek Rd, Poway, CA 92064
(619) 748-9248

North West

Deborah Deonigi
P.O. Box 1140, Maple Valley, WA 98038
(360) 886-7075 / (206) 735-3540 fax

Cleveland Johnson
Expository Bible Teaching
6616 Fenway Dr., Pasco WA 99301
(509) 544-0578

Judi Sato
Beautiful Gate Ministries
3834 SE Spruce St., Hillsboro, OR 97123
(503) 640-8028

South West

Carl Greer
2400 Lakeview Circle, Arlington, TX 76013
(817) 261-4435 / (817) 277-7803 fax

Toby Hooten, Pastor
Chama Community Church
P.O. Box 94, Chama, NM 87520
(505) 756-2515

Canada

Sylvain Gauthier
784 RR7, Ste- Clothilde, QU G0N 1C0
CANADA
(418) 484-5611

Rick Melvin
624 16 Street South
Lethbridge, AB T1J 3B2
Canada

Bryan Yager, Pastor
River of Life Community Church
205 Meadowbrook Rd RR #7
Victoria, BC V9E 1J5
CANADA
(604) 479-7166/ (604) 727-7826

Outside of the U.S.

Dr. Francis Agbana, Founder/Sr. Min.
Life Builders Intrn'l Network Min.
15 Porden Rd., London, SW2 5SA England
+44-171-978 fax

David Drew
20 Hulingham, South Perth, 6151
Western Australia
011-61-9-474-4904

Peggy Lee Kannaday
Chowon Apt # 602 (Soonbokeum)
Young-Deung-Po
Seoul, Yoido 11-1 150-010, Korea

MorningStar Publications

Call For These Free Catalogs:
- **Resource Catalog**
- **Audio & Video Tapes**
- **Bulletin & Journal Back Issues**

1-800-542-0278

MorningStar
PUBLICATIONS
16000 Lancaster Highway
Charlotte, NC 28277-2061

STATEMENT OF OWNERSHIP, MANAGEMENT, AND CIRCULATION (REQUIRED BY 39 U.S.C. 3685)

1. Publication Title: The Morning Star Journal.
2. Publication No.: Vol.6-No.4.
3. Filing Date: October 1, 1996.
4. Issue frequency: Quarterly.
5. No. of issues published annually: 4.
6. Annual Subscription Price: $12.95 U.S.; $20.00 Int'l.
7. Complete Mailing Address of known office of publication: 16000 Lancaster Highway, Charlotte, NC 28277-2061.
8. Complete mailing address of generaloffice: same as #7.
9. Publisher: MorningStar Publications, Inc. 16000 Lancaster Highway, Charlotte, NC 28277-2061;
   Editor: Rick Joyner, 16000 Lancaster Highway, Charlotte, NC 28277-2061.
   Managing Editor: Dianne C. Thomas, 16000 Lancaster Highway, Charlotte, NC 28277-2061.
10. Owner: MorningStar Publications, 16000 Lancaster Highway, Charlotte, NC 28277-2061.
11. There are no bondholders, mortgages or other security holders.
12. The purpose, function, and non-profit status of this organization has not changed during the preceding 12 months.
13. Publication Name: MorningStar Publications, Inc.   14. Issue Date for Circulation Data Below: July 1996.

	Average No. of Copies Each Issue During Preceding 12 Months	Actual No. of Single Issue Published Nearest to Filing Date
15. Extent and Nature of Circulation		
a. Total No. of Copies (Net Press Run)	25,335	31,140
b. Paid and/or Requested Circulation		
(1) Sales Through Dealers and Carriers, Street Vendors, and Counter Sales	--0--	--0--
(2) Paid or Requested Mail Subscriptions	18,059	20,693
c. Total Paid and/or Requested Circulation (Sum of 15b(1) and 15b(2))	18,059	20,693
d. Free Distribution by Mail	975	1,150
e. Free Distribution Outside the Mail	25	25
f. Total Free Distribution (Sum of 15d and 15e)	1,000	1,175
g. Total Distribution (Sum of 15c and 15f)	19,059	21,868
h. Copies Not Distributed		
(1) Office Use, Leftovers, Spoiled	6,277	9,272
(2) Return from News Agents	-- 0--	--0--
i. Total (Sum of 15h(1) and 15h(2))	25,335	31,140
j. Percent Paid and/or Requested Circulation (15c/ 15g x 100)	95%	95%

16. This Statement of Ownership will be printed in the Vol.6 No. 4 issue of this publication.

Dennis Rippy Business Manager August 14, 1996